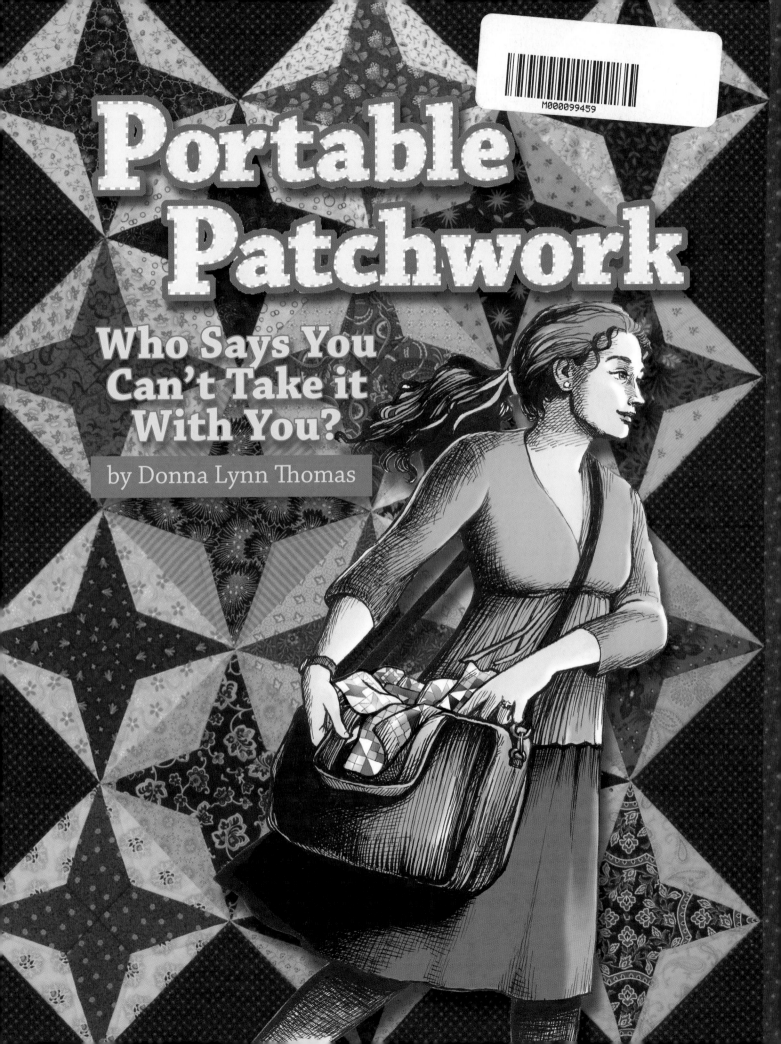

Portable Patchwork

Who Says You Can't Take it With You?

by Donna Lynn Thomas

Portable Patchwork
Who says you can't take it with you?
Author: Donna Lynn Thomas

Editor: Edie McGinnis
Technical Editor: Pamela Mayfield
Designer: Kelly Ludwig
Photography: Aaron T. Leimkuehler
Illustration: Lon Eric Craven
Production assistance: Jo Ann Groves

Published by:
Kansas City Star Books
1729 Grand Blvd.
Kansas City, Missouri, USA 64108

First edition, first printing
978-1-933466-51-4
Printed in the United States of America by Walsworth
Publishing Co., Marceline, Missouri

To order copies, call StarInfo at (816) 234-4636 and say
"Books."

 KANSAS CITY STAR BOOKS

www.PickleDish.com

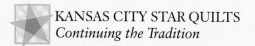
KANSAS CITY STAR QUILTS
Continuing the Tradition

Contents

YOU **CAN** TAKE IT WITH YOU!
Check out our special offer on the
Omnigrid Quilter's Travel Case, Page 128.

Dedication

This book is dedicated to the memory of Ann Woodward. Ann was a good friend and quilting buddy who gently passed away at far too young an age. She has been, and will continue to be, missed by many.

Acknowledgements

A book by its very nature is a group project. The members of the group come from far and wide.

First I would like to thank Mary Louise Kuslesza for finishing Ann's quilt for inclusion in my book. Ann and I had spoken the evening before she died about putting her new quilt in Portable Patchwork. I was devastated to get a different call the next day. Fortunately, Ann's mom, Mary Louise is an expert and talented quilt maker in her own right.

My good friends and fellow Army wives in the Leavenworth Prairie Chicks are so important. They made quilts, barnstormed ideas and gave me frank opinions and advice. Their friendship has been a godsend as always.

Thanks to Linda Harker, Doris Brown, Deb Rose and Kathy Brigham for making quilt samples for this book. I can always rely on my vast network of quilting friends for wonderful variations on my designs.

A big thank you goes to Nancy Wakefield for proofing the book for me before submission.

Aline Duerr has beautifully hand quilted many quilts for me over the years and special thanks always go to her. Denise Mariano finished the hand quilting on Piece in the Garden. Her work is lovely and I thank her from the bottom of my heart.

My quilts would not come to life without the invaluable contributions of the talented machine quilters I have come to know and value. Many thanks go to Charlotte Freeman, Kelly Ashton, Sandy Gore, Don Sutcliffe, Kim Pope, Freda Smith and Barb Fife. I have no talent for machine quilting and stand in awe of their abilities.

I have the absolute pleasure of working at Prairie Point Quilts in Shawnee, KS. Carol Kirchoff, the owner, and my fellow co-workers were a fountain of support and ideas. Never too busy to stop and help me, their friendship makes it a joy to go to work.

And last but not least, a book is never born without the far ranging talents of the production folks, photographer, and publisher. I owe many thanks to the staff at Kansas City Star Books; Doug Weaver, the publisher, who thought my book idea was a good one, my ever patient, witty and calm editor, Edie McGinnis, graphic artist, Lon Eric Craven for his precise illustrations, tech editor, Pam Mayfield, Jo Ann Groves, production assistant, page designer, Kelly Ludwig and Aaron Leimkuehler, photographer extraordinaire, for his "photo styling" and fun at the photo shoot. I can't thank these folks enough for the wonderful work they do giving birth to a brand new book!

Donna Lynn Thomas has been sewing since the age of four and quilting since she was in college over thirty years ago. Although she is the author of eight previous quilt titles teaching precision rotary cutting and machine piecing, her first and continuing love has been hand work. Her newest book, *Portable Patchwork*, published by *Kansas City Star Books*, reintroduces the low-tech hand-piecing skills of yesteryear and integrates them with new and modern machine skills. No longer tied exclusively to a sewing machine, modern quiltmakers can take their piecework on the go with them and once back home take that same project right back to the sewing machine. This integrated approach guarantees continued and versatile progress no matter where they happen to be. Of course, many quilters will discover what one of Donna's friends observed after hand piecing a project for the book, "I had forgotten just how much I really enjoyed hand-piecing! Now I look at all my projects with hand-piecing in mind."

Donna has been a certified National Quilting Association teacher for basic quiltmaking (NQACT) for 20 years. She has taught nationally and internationally and is the author of *Country Schoolhouse*, *Small Talk*, *Shortcuts* (imperial and metric versions, and four translations), *A Perfect Match*, *Shortcuts to the Top*, *Stripples*, *Stripples Strikes Again!*, *Scrappy Duos* and the designer of the Bias Stripper™ ruler. She has contributed articles on various quilt related subjects to a variety of publications over the years. Her most recent book, *Portable Patchwork* will be available in spring 2008.

Introduction

Too many times I hear quilters lament that once the weather turns nice or they are traveling, they have to give up their piecing. They close up shop for months because they are tied to their rotary cutters and sewing machines. This should not be so! Like knitting, crocheting, and cross-stitching, hand piecing used to be the ultimate portable needle art.

We modern quilters seem to have lost the low-tech skills that enabled our predecessors to take their piecework with them just about anywhere they went. Hands can fly while people talk.

Think of where piecework can go. The possibilities are endless—children's sports or activities, the pool, on the road in a car or RV, on the plane, train, cruise ship or bus, to the beach, quilting guild meetings, barbecues, hospital waiting rooms, or even as a patient yourself in some instances. Keep a small basket of your supplies close at hand and you're ready to go at a moment's notice.

Portability is not just for outside the home either. Picture a roaring fire on a cold winter's eve. The family is all gathered in front of the fire and you certainly do not want to be off in your sewing room. Bring your patchwork with you in front of that fire and enjoy the company of your family and some hot chocolate while still getting some piecing done. It's the best of both worlds.

Alternately, take it outside to the garden. There is nothing more exquisitely delightful than to steal a few minutes in the garden to slow down, sew a few stitches, and enjoy the peace and tranquility found there—no fast pace, no rush, just the fullness of the senses, gentle breezes, the warm sun and gently productive hands.

The process of hand piecing is by its very nature slower and there is a quiet pleasure in the process of constructing blocks a little bit here and a little bit there watching your designs slowly take shape and come together. There are also certain blocks I prefer to tackle by hand because I have more control over the process with my hand held needle as opposed to an electric needle.

On the other hand, one of the nice things about hand piecing is that it is not an all or nothing venture. With proper planning, you can take your piecing right back to the sewing machine and continue sewing without missing a beat. And surprisingly, there are a few tricks that enable you to take your rotary cut pieces right back to your hands when need be again. Versatility is the name of the game here—you CAN mix both methods all in one quilt.

My goal is to teach you the hand piecing skills that will make you a totally versatile quilter, able to integrate both hand and machine skills and move back and forth between the two worlds. With just a little practice, you will soon enjoy the world of Portable Patchwork.

Fabric Considerations

Your best fabric choice for quilt making is 100% cotton. We didn't always have the wonderful selection of high quality cottons and dyes available to us that we do now. The designer lines and huge variety of styles and looks give us unlimited potential for our quilts.

There are a few things to consider when planning a project that includes hand piecing. The overwhelming majority of 100% cotton quilt weight fabrics sew up beautifully by hand. In fact, some brands and styles are an absolute dream to piece while others are not.

For instance, we have a huge selection of beautiful designer flannels available to us today but I don't think I would choose to hand piece an entire quilt using only flannels. They are thick and not as malleable to work with for hand piecing. That's not to say I would not sew flannel—just maybe not use them for an entire quilt.

There are stunning batiks on the market too but you need to be aware that, for hand piecing, the fine, tight weave of these fabrics make them a little more difficult to sew. It's not an impediment for me but please be aware that they are more resistant to needles than regular cottons—the needle seems to drag a bit in a batik.

When considering hand woven fabrics for your projects, the finer weaves piece quite nicely but a looser or more open weave can cause a little trouble. By the same token, some of the very, very fine new cotton jacquards and other delightfully unique quilt fabrics we are seeing can be slippery, requiring more control than normal. None of these things are reason to discard a fabric, simply characteristics to be aware of when making your choices for a project.

Fabric Preparation

Whether you like a fixed palette or a scrappy, multi-fabric look for your quilts, all your fabrics should be prepared for cutting according to some basic guidelines.

I prefer not to pre-wash my fabric with a few exceptions. The sizing on the fabric contains a mildew retardant that I do not want to remove because I collect fabric and often store it for many years. But, if you are mixing fabrics of different weights such as wovens, batiks, flannels or regular cottons, they should all be washed to pre-shrink them. By the same token, if one of the fabrics you are using has been previously washed, the others should be also.

I test for bleeding by putting 3" squares of suspect fabrics in very hot water for 20 minutes. If bleeding occurs, I treat the yardage with Retayne and then pre-wash all fabrics going into the quilt. Do not wash your fabrics or finished quilts with detergents. Use quilt soap designed specifically for cottons. Detergents break down dye bonds in cotton fibers resulting in color fading and can potentially cause bleeding in the future as the bond weakens.

Once washed, dry your fabric on low heat until it is damp dry and then press it with a hot iron. If you dry it completely, creases set in harder. Refold the fabric as it came off the bolt, selvage to selvage, particularly if you will be rotary cutting. You may find that when lining up the selvages, the cut edges no longer match. This is fairly common. Shift the selvage edges along each other until the layers lie flat. If the yardage is not too long, you can do this easily by holding the fabric suspended from your hands with the selvages together. Shift the layers, while hanging, back and forth until the ripples disappear and the fabric is smooth. Press. If the yardage is too long to hold up comfortably, work on your ironing board a little bit at a time, aligning, smoothing and pressing.

Grain Line

There are three types of fabric grain. Yarns running parallel to the selvage are the lengthwise grain. This grain has little to no give. Yarns running perpendicular to the selvage are the crosswise grain and have a small amount of give. Patchwork edges cut parallel to either of these two grains are considered to be on the straight-grain. The bias grain runs at a 45° angle to the straight grain. Bias edges distort and stretch easily.

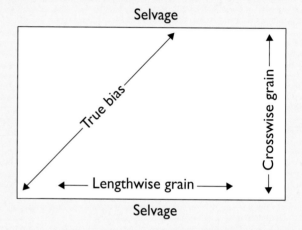

There are two rules to follow when trying to decide which edges to mark on the straight grain.

1. Place all edges that will be on the perimeter of a quilt block on the straight grain.

2. Whenever possible without violating rule #1, sew a bias edge to a straight grain edge to stabilize the bias.

Sometimes both rules are ignored in favor of design or other considerations. In such situations, tame the bias edge with a little spray sizing.

Hand Piecing

Basic Sewing Supplies

Hand piecing by its very nature is a relatively simple, low-tech process. As a result, there are not a lot of essential tools. There are many optional tools and gadgets to buy, and I certainly have bought my share, but the basics are simple and quite portable.

Sandpaper board

This is a rough surface board that can be homemade or purchased. We used to make them by gluing superfine sandpaper to a flat, stiff surface such as picture matting, artist's canvas or self-adhesive needlework mounting board. You can purchase ready-made boards now that have multiple functions. One has 3 surfaces; a rough surface for marking, a flannel piece to put on the rough surface for laying out pieces for sewing and a hard surface as a general purpose work area. It is a very convenient and portable multi-purpose surface.

Marking pencils

Lead pencils, whether regular or colored, are generally used for marking the wrong side of fabric. Chalk or wash-away pencils are used for marking the right side of fabric for appliqué or quilting marks. There are many products available. I prefer chalk for marking my appliqué and quilting as it comes out completely without any residual chemicals left in place to come back and haunt me later. Be sure to keep all your pencils sharp. NEVER use any type of ink anywhere on your quilt except the label.

Scissors

You need three types of scissors for hand piecing. The first is a good set of fabric shears that are used for nothing else. You also need a sharp set of craft scissors that can cut plastic cleanly. And last, you need a small pair of scissors for clipping threads. You can use your shears for this but I think you'll find them unwieldy for this function.

Seam Ripper

I hate to tell you that you need one but the reality is that you will at some point have to "reverse stitch"— a sad but true fact.

Threads

The thread for hand piecing should be fine (50-60 weight), strong (2-3 ply) and long staple 100% cotton. Do not use quilting thread for hand piecing. There are several brands of suitable hand piecing thread that I am pleased with; DMC® machine embroidery thread, Mettler®fine machine embroidery thread, and Prescencia® 50 or 60 weight cotton thread. The thread for piecing should be fine so it settles into the weave of the cotton fabric. This makes for a softer, finer, more supple seam with a better turn when pressing. I'm sure you can't imagine that a thick cord will settle between the finer threads of a cotton fabric making for a soft, supple seam. A fine thread will settle in though and that is what we want.

The thread should always be of the same fiber content as the fabrics and therefore, cotton covered polyester is inappropriate for cotton fabrics as it is stronger and will cut through the fabric with time. Thread should also be weaker than the fabric so, if under stress, the thread in the seam will break and not cut the fabric. Broken threads can be replaced but cut fabric cannot be fixed. Test your thread by snapping it firmly—it should offer some resistance before breaking.

I generally use shades of neutral for my piecing— grays and tans in varying degrees of dark and light depending on the fabrics I have chosen. The thread color should be neither darker than the darkest print, nor lighter than the lightest and I will vary it throughout the project, as need dictates. For instance, if I am sewing two dark prints together I will most likely use a very dark gray. When working with two light prints, I will switch to a light gray or cream-colored thread.

Needles

There are many types and brands of needles out there. When it comes to hand piecing, keep this in mind: you will not make small stitches with a crow bar and twine. My point is that fine stitches come from fine needles and fine high quality thread. I prefer to use size 12 quilting betweens for my hand piecing. They are short and fine and are the reason I can get tiny stitches. But I am a short person with small hands, which can make a difference. Some people prefer a type of needle called a sharp which is generally longer than a between but still fine in diameter. Both betweens and sharps come in sizes ranging from 9-12 with 12 being the smallest. Different manufacturers have different features with their sharps and betweens from gold eyes to larger eyes and on. I suggest you try a number of different needles and see which you prefer. Needles can be quite personal in selection and it may take a while for you to find your favorite.

Pins

There are two types of sewing pins that quilters generally use. You will need a good box of fine, glass head silk pins. They are sharp and slender and longer than appliqué pins. The glass heads are nice because it's easier to grab the pins to remove them. The downside is the sewing thread can catch in them more easily than the pins without the glass heads. Still I prefer them, as they are easier to grasp and remove. Silk pins are quite different from the quilting pins that are used to pin the three layers of a quilt sandwich together in preparation for basting. Quilting pins are large and completely unsuitable for hand piecing work.

Template Construction

Templates are pattern pieces transferred to durable material. Not too long ago our options were limited to paper, cardboard, exposed x-ray film and other items. None of these items were terribly convenient or appropriate because they wore out or were flimsy. These days we have several options ranging from gridded plastic to heat resistant Mylar to translucent plastic. I prefer unmarked translucent acrylic plastic that is available at most quilt or craft stores. It can be drawn on using a number two pencil and just as easily erased if a mistake is made.

Templates are made either with or without 1/4"

seam allowances included. For hand piecing, finished size templates are best, as we need to mark a sewing line on the wrong side of the fabric in order to know where to stitch. When machine piecing, templates include seam allowances so we can measure in 1/4" from the raw edge using the 1/4" guide on the sewing machine; no marked sewing line is needed. You will see most template patterns have two lines—one solid and one dotted line 1/4" outside the solid lines. Use the solid lines to make templates for hand piecing. Use the dotted lines to make templates for machine piecing.

To make templates, place the template plastic over the pattern to be traced. If it is a geometric shape, mark the points or corners of the shape only. Remember to mark either on the dotted or solid line depending on your plans. Using a rotary ruler or straightedge, connect the dots with lines. Use a fine line lead pencil and keep it sharp.

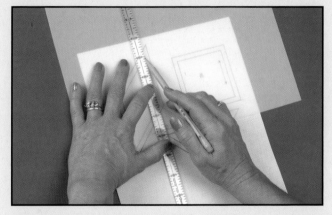

On the template write its designation (A, B, C or 1, 2, 3). Also transfer any matching marks or grain-line arrows to the plastic. Some quilters like to write the size of the template on it so they can reuse it later in another project that uses the same size shape. Mark on the right side of the template. The right side is the side face up as you trace. The distinction between right side and wrong side is important sometimes—you must be able to tell right side and wrong side after the template is cut by which side has the writing on it.

Be efficient in the use of your plastic when marking. It is okay to trace templates that share lines and cut them apart on that shared line—no need to waste the plastic. Now cut out the templates using sharp craft scissors and

a steady hand.

If the pattern is curved, first trace any straight edges as described above. Then, very carefully and slowly trace the curved edge(s) using small short movements.

Another method to make curved shapes is to photocopy the shape onto a piece of paper. Cut the shape from the paper outside the template lines.

Place dots of water-soluble glue stick on the wrong side of the cut paper inside the template area and stick it to the template plastic. Now cut out the template following the lines on the paper. Remove the paper from the plastic and wipe off the glue stick residue with a damp paper towel. Write the template designation and other information on the right side of the template.

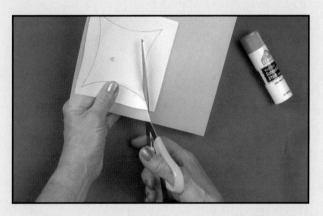

Always check all cut templates against the masters for accuracy. Adjust or remake any that are not perfect.

Generally when we prepare to trace around templates on fabric, we lay the templates right side down on the wrong side of the fabric. Remember I mentioned that templates have right sides and wrong sides? Here is why that is important. In this book and others you will sometimes see templates with designations such as this: A-AR. This designation is used for asymmetrical images. The AR indicates Template A—reversed. A reverse template is a template turned over and marked for the reverse image. Study the shape on the top of page 10. The shape is the same in both markings but one is the mirror image of the other. To produce A, the template is marked right side DOWN on the wrong side of the fabric. To produce AR the template is marked right side UP on the wrong side of the fabric.

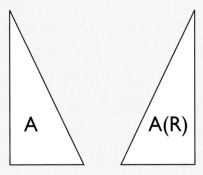

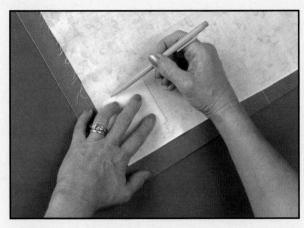

Marking Fabric

Sort all the templates to be marked and cut from the first one of your prints. Press the fabric smooth and lay it wrong side up on your sandpaper board with the selvage running from left to right in front of you. Start marking from the lower corner and work your way toward the opposite selvage. This is the most efficient way to mark your fabric. A rule of thumb is to always cut the largest pieces first and the smallest last. If you make a mistake at some point and come up short on fabric, it is easier to squeeze smaller shapes out of odds and ends as opposed to larger pieces.

Lay the first template you intend to mark right side down on the back of the fabric, unless it is a reverse template (see above). Align the grain arrow with either one of the straight-grains. Holding it firmly with one hand, trace next to the edges of the template carefully. Here are some tips:

◈ Use a fine line mechanical lead pencil or a very sharp #2 standard lead pencil.

◈ Hold the pencil at a 45° angle to the fabric to keep the point from dragging in the weave of the fabric. This also helps keep the pencil point sharp.

◈ Trace right next to the template along its edges but do not trace around the points. Instead, trace past them, creating a pair of crossed lines.

◈ Hold the template points firmly with your fingers to keep them from wobbling. Precision is key to marking the sewing lines.

◈ NEVER use any kind of ink to mark your fabric as it may bleed through now or sometime in the future.

◈ If you have trouble seeing lead pencil on the back of your fabric, try using #2 colored pencils such as Berol Verithin. Some chalk pencils work well also but they tend to be softer, break easily and must be sharpened frequently to keep a sharp point. If they are too chalky, they will brush away before you are done with them. Yellow, blue, pink or white will usually show on most dark prints.

When marking squares and rectangles, mark them neatly in rows and columns. Triangles can be marked in two ways depending on the grain arrows. Right triangles that have the grain line arrow on the short sides are called half-square triangles. Right triangles that have the grain line on the long edge are called quarter-square triangles. They are laid out and marked in two different ways because of their grain line needs. Study the illustrations below for ideas on efficiency.

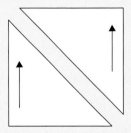 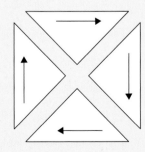

Mark all the templates to be cut from each of the prints you are using in your quilt on the correct prints.

Be careful not to get them mixed up. The written cutting instructions tell you which templates to mark and cut from which print.

. . . .
Cutting the Fabric

Once your fabric is marked, it is time to cut out the pieces. It is always a big question whether to add a cutting line or not. That is, do we mark a second line 1/4" away from the sewing line on which to cut? You can mark a cutting line with a ruler and pencil by drawing 1/4" away from the sewing line on all sides of the marked piece and cutting on the line with scissors. You can also use a rotary ruler and cutter to cut the pieces directly from the fabric without first marking a cutting line. Either way is fine and which method you use is usually determined by whether you have your rotary ruler and/ or other equipment available to use or not.

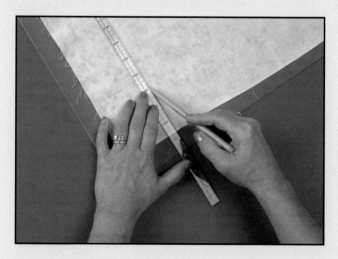

My general rule of thumb is that if the hand piecing will be mixed with machine piecing, I mark a cutting line if I am in a position to do so, for instance, at home with my rotary ruler and sewing supplies available to me. Of course, sometimes I may be at home but outside on a glorious day with absolutely no intention of going inside. In such cases, if I do not want to be bothered marking a cutting line, I tend to 'eyeball' and cut oversize seam allowances (slightly larger than 1/4") that I can rotary cut to a precise 1/4" later.

Another option when mixing hand and machine pieced blocks and units is to eyeball and cut only the

edges of the pieces that will lie on the outside of the block slightly oversized and eyeball a regular 1/4" for the interior edges. This way, all I have to do is trim the outside edges of the block to a nice, neat 1/4" seam allowance when it is done before attaching sashings or borders or whatever else I am planning to sew by machine. This is my preferred method when I know I will be mixing methods. It requires the least amount of equipment, which always matters to me when I am enjoying the hand process or am away from home.

On the other hand (so to speak!) if I plan to hand piece the entire quilt, I don't worry about a cutting line at all. In that case, I simply "eyeball" the distance and cut roughly 1/4" from the marked sewing lines. The sewing lines are all that matter in this case and over the years I have gotten pretty good at eyeballing that 1/4".

Quilt projects in this book such as the Simple Star quilts, Spring Fling, For Ann, Periwinkle, Mother's Stars in Heaven, and many others were assembled with all hand pieced blocks, trimmed to 1/4" on the edges when complete, and then sewn together with rotary cut and machine pieced borders.

Some quilts are composed of both hand and machine pieced blocks. Sometimes the blocks themselves mix both hand and machine pieced elements. In such cases, cut measured seam allowances. As you can see, these are choices for you to consider with your own projects—what you do will be unique to each particular situation.

. . . . . .
Pinning

Once your pieces are cut, it is time for the fun stuff. As you always should, lay out the pieces for one block on a flat surface or flannel board to make sure you have all your pieces and have cut everything correctly—especially if you are working with reverse templates. Now is the time to see if they are all the correct image, not later.

Notice the block assembly sequence, whether it is a four-patch, a nine-patch or some other form. Look at the blocks below to see different types of assembly sequences. The units making up the patches may be pieced but the bold lines indicate the patches that go into that block. Notice that not all the patches are squares either—sometimes they are pieced rectangles or triangles or use diagonal strip assembly sequences. Generally, we assemble smaller pieces into patches, join the patches to form rows, and sew the rows together to complete the block.

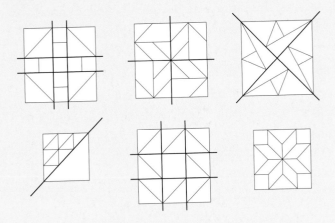

The purpose of pinning is to align the marked sewing lines on the two pieces to be sewn. Flip the two pieces right sides together along the edge to be sewn. Place a pin precisely in the first corner to be sewn working from the front side. Run the pin into the corner of the back piece exactly at its corresponding point. Do not secure it yet but rather leave it spearing the points. Repeat the process for the opposite corner on the other end of the seam to be sewn.

Once both corners are precisely speared, secure the pins in the fabric vertically taking a small bite of fabric. If the seam is more than an inch or two long, use the same spearing procedure to place another pin in the center of the seam, securing it vertically as well.

In order to ensure that the lines between the vertical pins line up a good bit of the distance, use horizontal pins to match the sewing lines along their length. Spear the front and back pieces at the same point and then secure the pin horizontally along the line turning the piece over to make sure the pin lies on the line on the back also. Place horizontal pins every 3-4 inches along the seam. If it is a short seam, it may need only the two corner pins and one horizontal pin. If it is really short, it may need only the vertical corner pins.

Threading the needle:

Cut your thread no longer than 12"-15". Any longer than this and the thread will wear out as it runs repeatedly back and forth through the eye of the needle.

Thread your needle from the end first off the spool. You will find the thread will snarl less due to the physics of the twist in the thread. An easy way to remember this is to thread the needle first and then cut it from the spool.

Sometimes it helps to cut the thread at an angle to make a small point at the end.

Unlike synthetic threads, you can moisten the end of a cotton thread to help the plies adhere to each other for easier threading.

Also, if you have difficulty threading your needle, turn the needle around. The eye of the needle is punched through the shaft of metal and therefore has a smooth side and a rough side.

When all else fails, use a needle threader to pull the thread through the eye of the needle.

Once the needle is threaded, leave a short tail and create a small knot on the long tail. The preferred knot is called a quilter's knot. Hold your needle up in the air with the thread dangling loose. Leave about half of the needle sticking up between your fingers. With your other hand, bring the long tail of the thread up in a circle to meet the point of the needle as if they were pointing at each other.

With the tail end and needle still pointing in opposite directions, grab them together between the thumb and forefinger of your sewing hand.

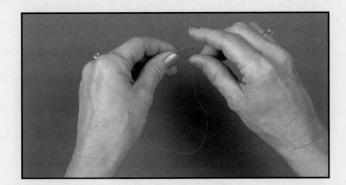

Using your non-sewing hand, tightly wrap the loop of thread around the point of the needle 3 or 4 times. Stop and, while still holding the wrapped thread tightly with the non-sewing hand, inch your sewing forefinger and thumb over the wrapping, keeping it tight and unraveled between your fingers.

Now using your non-sewing hand, pull the tip of the needle from between your fingers, while your sewing hand holds tightly to the wrapping. Pull the needle and thread all the way through the wrapped thread and your sewing fingers. Do not let go of the wrapped knot between your fingers until it reaches the end of the thread. Clip the tail to 1/4".

What you have done is make a small French knot on the end of your thread. It is a small, tight, true knot that will not come undone. It may take a little practice to master this knot but it is well worth the effort.

The Piecing Stitch

We sew with the piecing stitch. It differs from a basic running stitch in that we backstitch occasionally to make a stronger seam that is less likely to unravel if broken.

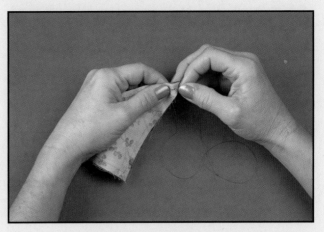

Beginning at the right corner if you are right-handed and the left corner if you are left handed, remove the first pin and take a stitch in the precise point where it held the corners. A stitch is the complete movement of the needle from front to back to front again. It should come up just a small distance away from where it started. Make a backstitch to secure the line of sewing by repeating that first stitch over again.

Now, this next part is a bit awkward when you are first learning but with practice it will become second nature just like any new skill. With your sewing hand, grab the corner layers of fabric between your forefinger and your middle finger and the needle between your thumb and forefinger.

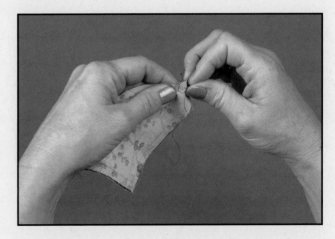

By holding the fabric end between those two fingers, you stabilize the fabric and use your thumb pad to hold the needle steady while weaving the fabric onto the needle with the other hand, pushing forward slightly with the sewing thumb at the same time. In fact, if you listen while I stitch you can hear my needle prick the forefinger of my non-sewing (receiving) hand on the bottom. As soon as I hear the prick, I know to pivot the needle up to catch the fabric as I weave the fabric onto the needle. I don't prick enough to draw blood!

Take your first needle full of stitches in this fashion. The first catch will be only a couple of stitches because it feels awkward and there is not much fabric to hold between your fingers. Once you pull that first couple of stitches through, you will have more fabric to grab and be able to take more stitches on each subsequent needle pull-through. It is important to take 4-6 or more stitches per pull through so that your stitches are straight. You will also develop a rhythm that will enable you to make smaller more even stitches with practice. Aim for about 8-10 stitches per inch. I sew at about 12 stitches per inch but I have been sewing for decades.

If you find your fingers become sore, particularly the pushing thumb and bottom receiving finger, there are protective pads available for just this purpose. I prefer the pads instead of thimbles because they still allow me to feel what is happening and likewise control and respond to my needle more closely.

After you pull each needle full of stitches through, begin the next needle full by making the first stitch right behind the last complete stitch, in effect making a backstitch. This backstitch at the beginning of each run of stitches is what distinguishes this from a simple running stitch. The piecing stitch is very difficult to unravel as opposed to a running stitch, which can be pulled right out of a seam.

Sew across the seam to the far corner and stop with your needle coming up precisely in this corner point. Make a backstitch by repeating the last stitch.

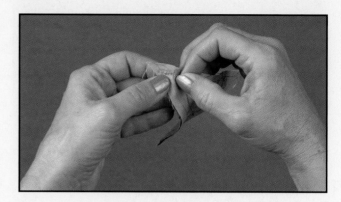

Make another stitch but don't pull it all the way through. Leave a small 1" loop. Run your needle and thread through the loop and pull the thread all the way through the loop without pulling the loop itself closed.

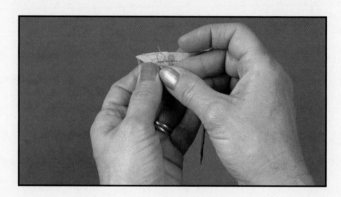

Now run the needle and thread through the loop a second time from the same direction as before. This time you can pull the loop closed. This forms a knot. Each seam is started with a knot and backstitch and ended with the reverse, a backstitch and a knot.

If you have cut oversized seam allowances, now is a good time to trim them back to a tidy 1/4" although, if not possible at this step, it can be done later. Generally it is easier to do it as you go, but since this may not be possible all the time, it is perfectly acceptable to wait.

Continue sewing smaller units of your block into patches with the goal of joining the patches into rows. At some point you will come across a seam with another seam intersecting it. We deal with that situation next in the section on *Free-Standing Seam Allowances*.

Free-Standing Seam Allowances

Now that you know the basic piecing stitch it is time to learn how to sew seams that cross previously sewn intersections without sewing the seam allowances down as we do when we piece by machine. There are a couple of advantages to leaving the seams flapping; the greatest benefit is that you can avoid sewing through all those layers of fabric from the seam allowances. My hands can't handle all that bulk like a sewing machine can! The second benefit is that we don't have to worry about pressing seam allowances in any particular direction until the block is complete, although I do like to finger press seams to keep the block from being too wild and out of control as the assembly process proceeds.

Begin in the same fashion as any seam, pinning outside points first. Then fold the seam allowance of the seam you need to cross out of the way in the direction away from where you will start stitching. Place a pin in the precise point of intersection at this seam and line it up with the sewing line on the back. Secure the pin vertically.

Place horizontal pins between the vertical pins as necessary. Knot, backstitch and sew a piecing stitch right up to the first intersection. Backstitch precisely in the intersection.

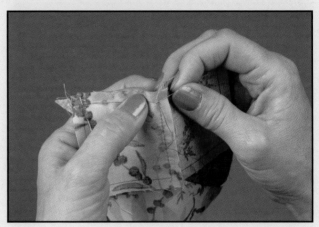

Run your needle through the base of the seam allowance and backstitch in the point on the other side. Look at the back side of the seam you are sewing. Those two backstitches should be sitting right next to each other forming a tight point where the pieces all meet. Continue stitching across the seam finishing the seam as usual with a backstitch and knot.

If there are two seams intersecting at one point, the process is almost exactly the same with one addition. Pin as above. Sew up to and backstitch in the intersection. Instead of running through the base of the seam allowance on the top, you are going to run your needle through the base of all the seam allowances. Begin by running your needle to the back of the work on the side of the seam you just backstitched. Pierce right through the point on the back but don't catch any seam allowance in your needle.

Now run the needle through the base of the seam allowance on the back side of the seam. Be precise!

Finally, bring your needle back to the front of your work on the opposite side of the top seam allowance. Pull the thread so it is snug and backstitch in this point and continue on your way stitching the seam as usual.

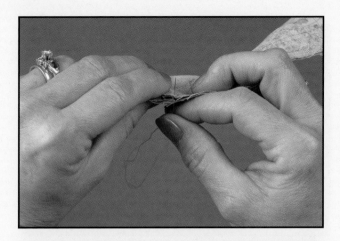

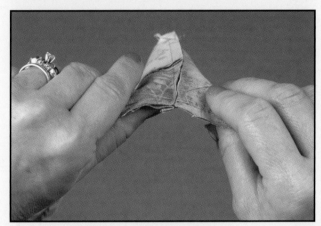

What you have done is drawstring that intersection like a cord in a laundry bag. You should see a nice tight, perfect intersection of points when you open your pieces up to the right side. Use this drawstring approach anytime you have multiple seams meeting at one spot.

Basic Rotary Cutting and Machine Piecing

Even though the meat and potatoes of this book is hand piecing, it is still important to review the basics of rotary cutting and machine piecing in order to understand how to integrate them with hand piecing. There are scores of books on the market that delve into many creative and advanced applications and uses of rotary cutting and machine piecing. This book is not about all of that. We will stick to the basics.

Rotary Cutting

Basic Rotary Cutting Equipment

You could spend a fortune and a lifetime acquiring rotary cutting gadgets and I am well on my way to winning that race. But, despite that, the essentials are all that are needed for most projects.

Rotary Cutters

Rotary cutters are round-bladed cutting tools used to cut fabric instead of shears. They come in all shapes and sizes and colors. There are even cutters with ergonomic handles for arthritic quilters. Rotary cutters are extremely sharp cutting instruments that must be treated with a great deal of care to avoid accidents. Please keep these tools well out of the reach of children—they can easily sever tiny fingers. Keep the safety shield engaged when you are not actually cutting with it.

Replace the blade when it begins to get dull as it can damage a rotary cutting mat. It also becomes more difficult to cut your fabric accurately. It helps to clean your blade periodically by dismantling your cutter and wiping it with a clean soft cloth. At the same time, put a tiny drop of sewing machine oil on the blade behind the sheath to keep it moving smoothly.

Rotary Mats

Rotary mats are special mats designed for use with

rotary cutters. Do not cut on any surface other than a special rotary mat or you will immediately ruin the blade of the cutter as well as the surface on which you cut. They come in many sizes and colors with various features touted as advantages. Most have a measuring grid on one side and are blank on the reverse. Please be aware that these measurements should never be used for precision cutting. Use them for rough cuts or cutting that does not require absolute precision.

Do not store or expose your mat to extreme temperatures. Heat will irreparably warp the mat while cold will make it brittle. They are fussy that way—no hot mugs or irons please.

You need a mat that is no smaller than 18" x 24" to cut properly. If you can afford one, the larger 24" x 36" is best for home use. I have both sizes, the larger for home and the smaller for classes.

Rotary Rulers

There is a ruler for every technique but the most important ones are the ones you use for routine cutting. I recommend several in different sizes, both square and rectangular to cover multiple functions. No matter what sizes you decide you need, you should look for some essential features.

◈ Transparent 1/8" hard acrylic plastic

◈ 1/8" markings on the 1" gridlines both horizontally and vertically and even more is better—one of my favorites has a 1/8" grid all over

◈ A "window" at each 1" intersection to help ensure that the edge of your fabric is where it should be in relation to the markings.

◈ Lines indicating 30°, 45° and 60° angles

• • • • • • • • • • • • • •

Basic Rotary Cutting

As you learned in Section I, when we cut fabric for hand piecing with templates, we mark sewing lines using templates and then cut 1/4" seam allowances past the marked line. Unlike hand piecing, there are no templates or marked sewing lines when rotary cutting and machine

piecing. All the pieces are measured and cut directly from the fabric using a ruler with the seam allowances included in the cut dimensions. Therefore the sizes listed in rotary cutting patterns are cut size. This is important to remember and distinguish from the finished size we prefer for hand piecing.

Creating a Clean-Cut Edge

Before you begin cutting, press your prepared fabric (whether pre-washed or not) smooth and refold it selvage-to-selvage right sides out the way it came off the bolt. If you are right handed you will be cutting your fabric from left to right. If you are left-handed you will cut from right to left.

◈ Lay the pressed fabric on the rotary mat with the fold toward you and the selvages at the top of the mat. Some quilters like myself, who are shorter, prefer to fold the fabric a second time with the bottom fold pressed up to the selvage edge for four layers. The shorter distance makes it easier to control the ruler while cutting and shorter arms have more power to cut firmly across the shorter distance. Other quilters need the extra fold in order to fit the fabric on their mat or under a 12" ruler. Whatever the reason, be sure to smooth the fabric and make sure the layers within the fold are neatly and closely aligned.

◈ Place the edge of your rotary ruler inside the raw edge of your fabric. If you are right-handed this will be the left side. If you are left-handed this will be the right side of your fabric. In order to make a cut that is at right angles to the fold, lay one edge of a second ruler on the fold of the fabric and adjust your cutting ruler so that it is flush with the ruler on the fold.

◆ Hold the ruler firmly with a downward pressure and your fingers spread wide to stabilize the ruler so it doesn't shift.

◆ While holding the cutting ruler stable, push the right angle ruler out of the way. Disengage the safety shield on the cutter, place the blade next to the ruler's edge below the lower fold, and begin to cut slowly away from yourself with firm, downward pressure. If your fabric is folded only once into two layers instead of four, you may need to periodically stop and slowly and carefully 'walk' your hand up the ruler without letting the ruler slip.

◆ Cut completely past the selvages and engage the safety mechanism before putting the cutter down. This newly clean-cut edge is your straight-grain cutting edge. You will begin cutting from this side.

◆ The purpose of this two-ruler method is so you don't move your fabric at all which can cause shifting and misalignment of the edges.

Cutting Strips, Squares and Rectangles

◆ The strip is the basic unit of rotary cutting. Once you have a clean-cut edge you can begin cutting strips. If you are right-handed, measure in and cut from the left edge. If you are left-handed, measure and cut from the right side. Directions for left-handed quilters are in parentheses where a difference occurs.

◆ Measure in the correct distance from the right (left) edge of the ruler and align this measurement line on the clean edge of the fabric.

◆ In addition, align one of the horizontal ruler lines on the bottom fold so the ruler is at right angles to the fold. This prevents the creation of a bent or angled strip when you unfold it after cutting.

◆ Cut strips from bottom to top just as you did when creating the clean-cut edge.

You may find after several cuts that you need to recreate a new clean-cut edge because you can no longer line up a ruler on the bottom fold and along the cutting edge at the same time. Do not be alarmed—this is normal as there is usually a miniscule amount of slippage with each cut that escalates into misalignment at some point.

To crosscut the strip into smaller strip lengths, squares or rectangles, first remove the selvages. Then lay the strip out as shown in the photo. Measure in from the short edge along the length of the strip the desired distance and cut. It is always a good idea to have a horizontal line on the long edge, again to ensure a right angle cut. You don't want drunken squares and rectangles that don't stand up straight.

Cutting Right Triangles

We use right triangles quite extensively in our patchwork designs. There are two types of triangles, which are created by cutting squares differently. We cut the squares differently in order to place the straight-grain on either the short edge of the triangles or the long edge.

Half-square triangles are right triangles created by cutting a square on its diagonal once. This yields two triangles with the straight-grain on the short edges.

To compute the size square to cut, add 7/8" to the desired finished size of the short edge of the half-square triangle. For example, if you want a 2" finished size half-square triangle, cut a 2 7/8" square. Cut it in half once on the diagonal, yielding two triangles. Once all seams are sewn, each triangle will finish to 2".

You will often see this symbol ◹ used in cutting instructions. It tells you to cut the square(s) you just made once diagonally to create half-square triangles.

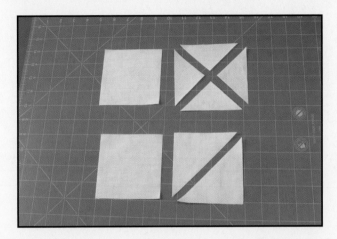

Quarter-square triangles are also right triangles. Cut a square on both diagonals to create four right triangles that have the straight-grain on the long edge.

To compute the size of the square to cut, add 1 1/4" to the finished size of the long edge of the triangle. If you want a triangle that measures 3" finished size on its long edge, cut a 4 1/4" square. Then cut the square on both diagonals to create four triangles.

You will often see this symbol ⊠ used in cutting instructions. It tells you to cut the square(s) you just made twice diagonally to create quarter-square triangles.

· · · · · · · · · · · ·

Cutting Odd Shapes

It is possible to combine templates and the rotary cutter to cut odd shapes from your fabric. Begin by making templates with seam allowances added all around. As you would with hand piecing, trace carefully around the template on the wrong side of your fabric, near the bottom of the fabric yardage. I usually mark the shape twice, one right next to each other in an efficient

layout as shown in the photo. I then fanfold up to 6-8 layers of fabric under the template. Pin lightly to keep the layers from shifting. Place the rotary ruler on the marked line and cut the pieces from the fabric layers all at the same time using a sharp rotary cutter .

If your template is a reverse or asymmetrical template, then you cannot fanfold your fabric layers. Cut squares of fabric slightly larger than your first markings and layer them all under the marked area facing in the same direction.

· · · · · · · · · · · ·

Machine Piecing

Before you sew a stitch, check your machine to make sure it is in good working order. Clean and oil it according to your manual and put in a fresh needle. A Universal size 80/12 sewing machine needle is generally accepted for machine piecing for quilts. High quality 50-weight cotton, long staple thread that does not lint is best. There are many on the market. If you are new to quilting, ask your local quilt shop for advice or consult with a guild, experienced quilter or quilting internet site for reliable advice.

· · · · · · · · · · · ·

The Strip Test

As discussed earlier in the book, when marking with templates for hand piecing we draw a sewing line using finished size templates and then cut a measured 1/4" seam allowance away from the line. The sewing lines are matched and stitching is done on the lines.

With rotary cut pieces, the 1/4" seam allowances are built in and there are no marked sewing lines. In this case, when sewing by machine, we match raw edges and measure in a precise 1/4" from the edges and stitch. Absolute precision is necessary for the pieces to fit together. If the seam you take is too wide, the finished sizes of the pieces will be too small. On the other hand, if the seam you take is too narrow, the finished size of the pieces will be too big. Either way, your block is not going to fit together easily, resulting in a good bit of frustration.

Therefore, all the accurate cutting in the world won't mean a thing if your machine piecing is not accurate. Many people assume the edge of their standard presser foot is 1/4" wide. That is not true. As a result, most machine manufacturers have special 1/4" quilter's feet for their machines. Still it is a good idea to check the accuracy of the foot and your ability to use it properly! Conduct this simple test to see how you and your machine are doing.

◈ Cut 3 strips of fabric, each 1 1/2" x 3" in size.

◈ Sew the strips together side by side, using the 1/4" guide or foot for your machine. Be sure to align the raw edges carefully and evenly. Sew slowly and carefully using your best stitching.

◈ Press seams away from the center strip.

◈ Measure the width of the center strip using a 1"-wide ruler by laying the ruler in the channel formed by the center strip. It should fit on top of that center strip, snugly nestled against the ridges of the seam allowances. If there is any play in the ruler side to side, your strip is too wide, meaning your seam allowance is too narrow. If the ruler does not fit in the channel, your seam is too wide.

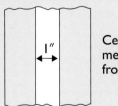

Center strip should measure a perfect 1" from seam to seam

Now turn the strips over. When you sewed, were the raw edges properly and evenly aligned? Did you follow your guide accurately? Did you taper in or out at the start or end of a seam? If you answered yes to any of these questions, you may be the culprit, not the machine and its guide. Redo the test being more careful. Continue practicing on strip sets until you have tamed your bad habits.

If you are not the problem and your sewing machine is a newer model, it may have multiple needle positions for zigzag stitching that allow you to move the needle in increments to the left and right of center. Try shifting your needle either to the left to widen your seam or to the right to narrow it and conduct another strip test. Continue testing needle positions until you find one that works accurately.

If all else fails, you will need to make a sewing guide on your throat plate.

◈ Cut a 2" x 6" piece of 1/4" grid graph paper.

◈ Put the graph paper under the presser foot and lower the needle into it on the first 1/4" line in from the right edge of the paper. Adjust the paper so it runs in a straight line from the needle towards you and is not slanted to either the right or left. You can often use other lines on the throat plate as guides for this.

◈ Lower the presser foot to hold the paper in place. If necessary, place a piece of tape on the left side of the paper to keep it from shifting on you.

◈ Place a piece of masking tape along the right edge of the paper in front of the needle area. Make sure it is in front of and out of the way of the feed dogs.

◈ Redo the strip test to determine the accuracy of this new guide. If it is not accurate, adjust it until you can conduct an accurate strip test. Once located, build up the guide with layers of masking tape or adhesive back foam. This provides a nice ridge along which to guide your fabric into the needle. Some quilters like this ridge even if their sewing foot is accurate. If nothing else, it is a good training tool to learn how to place your fabric perfectly to run it under the presser foot.

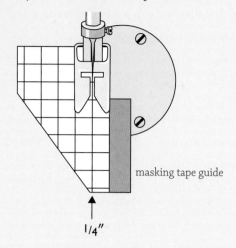

masking tape guide

1/4"

Sewing Rotary Cut Pieces

Machine piecing is the process of sewing two pieces of fabric together with a straight running stitch. Use the standard stitch length of 12 stitches per inch or the equivalent on your machine.

Since seam allowances are included in rotary cutting, raw edges are aligned in preparation for sewing. Rarely do we use pins to hold the pieces together, except in special circumstances. Generally, we do not backstitch at the beginning or end of each seam as every seam will be crossed and sewn down by another seam all the way out to the edges of the quilt.

Lift the presser foot slightly, place the beginning of the matched edges under the foot and begin stitching, sewing completely from the raw edge of one side of the seam to the other. Machine piecing may be faster but it is not a race. Fast stitching will most likely be sloppy stitching. Slow down and take your time to do it right the first time.

Nubbing Triangle Points

Many times we sew triangles to square corners. When this is the case, it is more accurate to nub or square off the ends of the triangles to neatly match the corners.

To nub half square triangles, determine the finished size of the short edge of the triangle by subtracting 7/8"

from the cut size. Now add 1/2" to the finished size to get the nubbing size. For example, a 3 7/8" cut size half-square triangle has a finished size of 3" (3 7/8" - 7/8" = 3"). Add 1/2" to 3" to get a nubbing size of 3 1/2". Use a square ruler or the corner of your rectangular ruler to measure this distance from the corner of the triangle and trim the points. Place the ruler measurement of the nubbing size on the corner of the triangle. The points will extend past the ruler. Trim them away and your triangle is nubbed. If you carefully stack your triangles, you can accurately nub four to six triangles at a time.

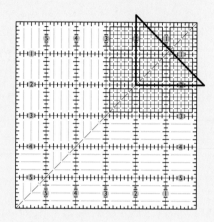

To nub quarter-square triangles, determine the finished size of the long edge of the triangle by subtracting 1 1/4" from the cut size. Divide this measurement in half and add 1/4". This is the nubbing size. As an example, a 4 1/4" cut size quarter-square triangle has a finished size of 3" (4 1/4" - 1 1/4" = 3"). Divide 3 in half to get 1 1/2". Add 1/4" to this to get the nubbing size of 1 3/4".

Before nubbing, fold the triangle in half along its long edge up to the right angle corner as in the diagram.

Do not cut upper tip of fold

Fold line

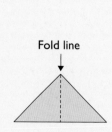

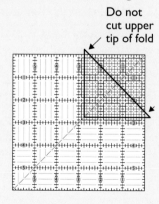

Now lay the nubbing measurement and the ruler on the folded edge of the triangle. Trim the points that stick out past the ruler to the right. Do not trim the folded point sticking out of the top of the ruler!! I recommend that you nub quarter-square triangles one at a time.

Matching Intersections

The best way to tightly match intersecting seams, is to make sure the two seams are pressed in opposite directions. This is called 'butting' or 'nesting' the seams. The ridges of the two seams can be fit tightly against each other resulting in a perfect intersection. This concept of butting seams works equally well for the diagonal seams of two pairs of triangles that intersect to form a point.

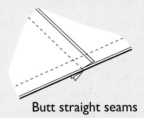

Butt straight seams

Sometimes it is necessary to plan the direction you will press your seams in advance. You can do this by sketching your block on paper in pen. Then with erasable pencil you can play with different pressing scenarios until you find one that enables you to butt matching seam intersections. This is called a pressing plan or guide.

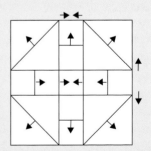

Many pattern writers, including myself, include arrows in our assembly diagrams that guide you in pressing your seams properly. Follow these directions scrupulously and you should find all your intersections nesting, although sometimes it is not possible to do so. In that case, we usually indicate the best solution we can.

Scrap Leads

This is a wonderful trick I learned in 1987 in a class with Jeannette Muir. Rather than starting each seam with loose thread tails that must be held tight, begin by sewing across a folded strip of fabric. It only needs to be about 1" wide. This is especially valuable if your machine's first few stitches tend to be rough, or you take a few stitches to get your accuracy on track, or if your machine tends to eat the beginning of each seam but calms down once it has fabric under the presser foot. It's better to have all these things happen on scraps. When I lived and taught in Germany, my students pointed out to me another big advantage to the use of scrap leads. Thread was quite expensive and by using these scrap leads, significant thread was saved since all those tails at the start and end of each seam were eliminated when used in combination with the chain-sewing concept discussed below.

Scrap lead

Chain Sewing

Chain sewing is an assembly line approach to piecing that saves time by sewing as many seams as possible one right after the other.

Begin with a scrap lead and continue feeding in as many matched pairs of seams as you have available. Leave a small twist of thread between each pair. End by sewing across another scrap of fabric and stopping with your needle down in the lead. Do not remove the scrap lead from under the needle. Clip the chain of piecing off the back of the scrap lead. With the scrap still in place, you will be ready to start another chain of piecing and will seldom have to deal with thread tails again. Clip the thread twists between each seam to separate your pieces.

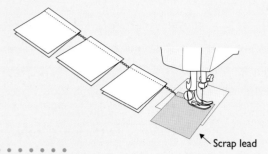

Scrap lead

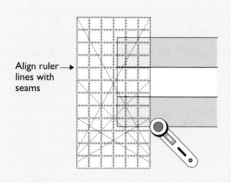

Align ruler lines with seams

Strip Piecing

This is a technique that came into full flower with rotary cutting and machine piecing. It was done before the advent of rotary cutters by tearing strips but wasn't too widespread. The idea is to sew strips of fabric together side by side and then cut them into segments of predetermined widths to create presewn units. It can eliminate the need to cut individual squares and rectangles that are destined to be sewn into larger units with other squares and rectangles.

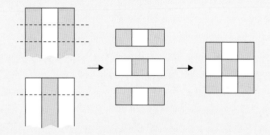

Cut strips the length indicated in your pattern. Sew them together side by side being careful not to tug on them and stretch them. Press each seam before sewing the next strip in place.

To cut segments from the strip unit, first trim one end even and at right angles to the seams. Then measure in and cut segments the appropriate width, always keeping a horizontal ruler line on the seams to keep the cuts at right angles. If you need to trim up the end to get back to right angles, do so.

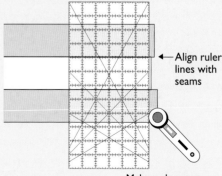

← Align ruler lines with seams

Make a clean cut

Quick Triangles

This simple technique helps make perfect pieced squares from half-square triangles without actually having to cut any triangles. The benefit of this method is the long bias edge is stabilized since it is kept within the confines of a square while sewing.

Pieced square

◆ From each of the two prints composing the pieced square, cut a square 7/8" larger than the desired finished size of the pieced square.

Finished size of pieced square

◆ On the wrong side of one of the squares, mark a diagonal line precisely across the center of the square from corner to corner. Next mark two more lines, each 1/4" on either side of the diagonal line. Place the marked square right sides together on top of the unmarked square. Pin them at each corner.

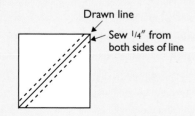

Drawn line

Sew 1/4" from both sides of line

◈ Sew on each of the 1/4" lines. Cut the square apart on the diagonal line between the stitching and press the pieced squares open. You will produce two pieced squares from every pair of squares you sew.

As an alternative, there are several brands of 1/2"-wide rulers available with lines running through the center that eliminate the need for the first drawn line. Place the center line of the ruler on the diagonal of the square precisely from corner to corner. Draw a line on either side of the ruler. Sew, cut and press as above.

Another way to achieve the same results is to mark only the center diagonal line, and then sew 1/4" on either side of the line using your 1/4" machine guide. Cut and press as above.

Folded Corners

Another shortcut technique, the goal of folded corners is again to avoid working with individual triangles and their pesky bias edges. We use many block units that have triangles sewn onto base shapes such as

the units below. There is a bit of waste in the process but the success of the technique often makes that justifiable.

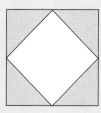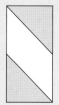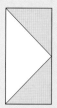

Begin by drawing a diagonal line across the back of the smaller square. Place the square right sides together on the corner of the square or rectangle, orienting the line to cut across the corner, not point into it. Pin the square at each corner and sew on the line.

Draw diagonal line

Stitch on drawn line

Fold the small square over the corner of the larger unit (hence the name, folded corners) to check to make sure it has been sewn accurately. If it is too big or falls short of the corner, adjust the seam as needed. Many people see improved accuracy when they just barely sew to the inside of the line on the side closer to the corner. Think of it as sewing on the side of the line, not down the center of the line; after all a line has a thickness, and you want to stitch on the side of the line closest to the corner. This allows a little give for the thickness of the fabric when it is folded over. Once the corner square is sewn in place properly, trim away the excess layers behind it to 1/4" from the seam line.

Fold square over corner

When sewing multiple corners on one base unit,

sew opposite corners first followed by the remaining two corners. Press each seam and trim the excess before sewing another seam that will cross it.

If you have trouble with your fabric slipping while you stitch, try placing a small dab of water-soluble glue-stick between the corner layers.

To determine the size pieces you need for folded corners, you need to know the desired finished sizes of the completed unit and the corner units. Add 1/2" to the finished sizes to calculate cut sizes. Look at the example in the diagram.

◆ The completed square within a square unit is 4" with the corner squares meeting in the center on each side.

◆ Therefore, the finished size of the folded corners is 2" (one half of 4").

◆ Add 1/2" to 4" base size and 1/2" to 2" finished size folded corner square.

◆ Cut 1- 4 1/2" base square and 4- 2 1/2" squares for the folded corners.

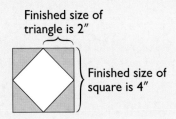

Finished size of triangle is 2"

Finished size of square is 4"

Specialty Seams

You have learned the basics of hand piecing. We have reviewed the basics of rotary cutting and machine piecing. Those basic skills will cover you in most cases but there are a few other special skills that are good to know so you are ready to tackle any block you wish to make without fear.

Set-in Seams

Set-in seams are seams that are sewn with a Y-construction process. I hear many long-time quilters express fear of this seam, which makes me chuckle.

Whether you sew by hand or machine, the process is essentially the same with a few minor adjustments. The only difference is whether you are sewing with a hand-held needle or a machine-guided needle.

Set-in seams are not difficult if you picture and treat each part of the seam as a single seam. In the diagram, the squares and triangles must be 'set-in' to the spaces between the diamonds in order to square off and finish the block

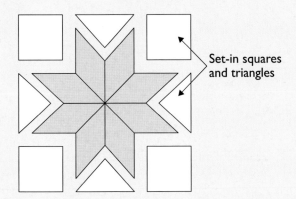

Set-in squares and triangles

For both machine and hand piecing, begin by laying one side of the square over the corresponding diamond edge to which it is to be sewn. Pretend this is the only part of the square you are sewing. Pin the edges together as normal. For rotary cut pieces, you should make a pencil mark 1/4" from each corner so you know where to stop and start.

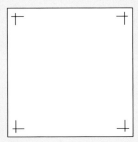

Mark 1/4" on all corners for rotary cut pieces

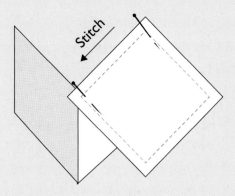

By Hand

Knot, backstitch and sew across the seam to the inside corner point as usual. Backstitch in the corner. Do not break the thread.

Put your needle out of the way by lodging it in the seam allowance then pivot the square so the next edge to be sewn is aligned with the adjacent diamond. It will pull and distort the piece you just sewed but that is fine.

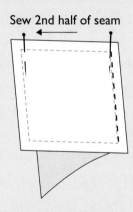

Slide your needle through the base of the seam allowance you just sewed to the starting point on the new seam. Again, treat this new seam as an individual seam, pinning, backstitching and sewing from the center point to the far side as you would with any simple seam. If this were the only set-in seam to sew, you would finish with a backstitch and knot and clip your thread.

If, as in the sample, there are more set-in seams on the entire perimeter of the block, do not break the thread. Instead, lodge your needle out of the way and pin the next triangle to its first side to be sewn. Slip the needle through the base of the seam allowance and sew

the first triangle seam as normal.

Continue in this fashion, sewing set-in seams with a continuous thread. When it is time to cut a new thread, make the change at an outside seam. Begin your new thread and knot on the end of the seam you just finished so you can run your needle through the base of the seam allowance to backstitch and start the next seam. The reason for this is to pull the squares and triangles at the outside edge tightly together so there is no gap where they meet.

By Machine

Pin and align the first seam as described with hand piecing above. Stitch from the inside point first, sewing toward the outer raw edge. Backstitch and cut the thread. The process for machine piecing set-in seams is the same as for hand piecing except that, unlike hand piecing, the machine-pieced seam will not be a continuous seam. Stop and start each individual seam separately, sewing from the center out.

Curved Seams

Many quilters are frightened by curves as well as set in-seams. Again, they are not nearly as scary as their reputation. They often are one of those slap-in-the-head things, where you find it just wasn't so bad after all. Of course, there are a few tricks and considerations that make it work well. The process is the same whether you are working by hand or machine, since most likely you have used templates to mark and cut your curved pieces. The only difference is that by machine you match raw edges if there is not a marked sewing line.

First some concepts; there are two types of curves in each curved seam, the concave curve and the convex. Remember them from geometry class? (Yikes—we actually use that stuff!) The concave curve bends inward (like walking into a cave) and the other, the convex curve, bends out. The idea of making them fit to each other is what some find scary.

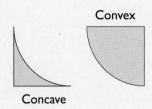

Convex

Concave

First, mark the center of each seam. Most curved templates have a slash mark on them at the center of the seam. Transfer that mark to the center of the sewing line in the seam allowance. If your templates do not have a center mark, press one into the seam. Fold the seam in half, matching points, and finger pressing a crease in the center of the sewing line. For reasons you will soon understand, I press my concave piece with right sides together and the convex piece with wrong sides together. Now make short clips into the seam allowance of the concave piece only. Do not cut into the sewing line but just up to it. I begin with clips every half inch or so. The deeper the curve, the more clips are needed but it's best to start with fewer clips and add more as needed than to overdo it from the start.

When you lay out the pieces flat along their matching seams in preparation for pinning, it doesn't look like there is any way that they are going to fit together but believe me, they do. I find it helpful to pin the concave piece TO the convex piece, i.e., the convex piece is right side up on the bottom when I start pinning.

Ignore the curvature of the seam and pin the two outside corners and the inside center marks or pressings. If you have pressed the concave piece right sides together and the convex piece wrong sides together, you will find the creases cup together nicely as the creases fold in the same direction; a small but convenient detail.

Now, begin pinning between the corners and center pin, working in small sections, stretching the top piece to fit over the bottom piece. Pin the center of each section, then the center of each of those halves, slowly pinning new centers until the pieces fit nicely. The clip marks help the concave fabric stretch around the convex piece. In fact, I find it helpful to let the bottom piece curve around and down while I fit the top piece over it. They cooperate better when you allow them to fall into a downward curve. Pin heavily and secure all pins vertically.

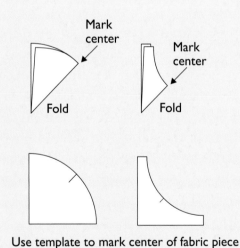

Mark center

Fold

Mark center

Fold

Use template to mark center of fabric piece

Make clips along concave curves

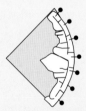

Pin concave piece to convex piece with center guidelines matching

By Hand

Sew the seam as you would any seam, only removing the pins just as you get to them. Take fewer stitches on your needle. Sew slowly, checking the back before each needle pull through to make sure you are staying on both lines. The slowness and heavy control of this process is why I prefer to sew curved seams by hand. Machines are so fast that errors are locked in before you can fix them.

By Machine

Sew slowly and carefully. Measure carefully from the raw edges if you are working without marked sewing lines. Take shorter stitches so the seam is smooth and even.

Multiple Center Seams

There are many beautiful star and spinning designs that involve many seams converging at one point in the center. In order for these seams to meet precisely without gaps, you must practice precision at each step of the way. Of course, you should do this with all of your piecing but central seams have a way of highlighting shortcomings. I have a few tricks that may help.

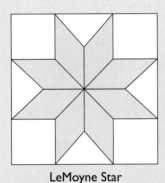

LeMoyne Star

Using the LeMoyne Star as a sample, we see there are 8 diamonds that all meet in the center. Making precise templates, marking and cutting carefully, and pinning seams exactly will go a long way to making a perfect star. Unfortunately, all that backstitching and knotting at the junction of the center points can cause a build up of bulk in the center resulting in lumpiness and inaccurate looking points.

To avoid bulk, try a different strategy for locating knots and backstitching. Pin a pair of diamonds together as you would normally.

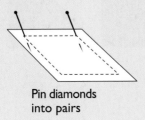

Pin diamonds
into pairs

By Hand

Pin and sew from the outside edge toward the center as you would with any seam. At the inside point, backstitch once. Then backstitch and knot just above the end of the seam in the seam allowance instead of on the seam itself. Cut the thread. This reduces the bulk of many knots all meeting in the center of the star.

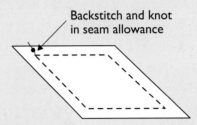

Backstitch and knot
in seam allowance

Continue sewing the diamonds together into pairs and the pairs into half-blocks. Sew the final seam joining the half-blocks, leaving free-standing seam allowances in the center. Press the seams in a circular fashion to evenly distribute the bulk. The seams on the back in the center should form a little pinwheel on the wrong side. This distributes the bulk of the points evenly and can only be accomplished with free-standing seam allowances in the center.

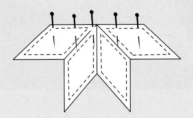

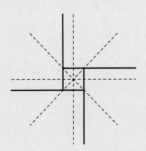

By Machine

Follow the same process as above. Begin your first stitching by arranging your piece under the needle with the seam allowance to the left of the needle. Begin stitching in the seam allowance and sew into the center point, stopping with the needle down in the point, pivoting, then sewing the seam out to the outside edge. Cut the thread as usual. Complete the star as with hand piecing, by sewing diamonds into pairs and pairs into halves, pressing in a clockwise direction as you go. When you reach the point of sewing the halves together, all center seams should butt when matching the final seam. Spear the center point with a pin but do not secure it in the fabric—just leave it sticking up. Now, place a pin about 1/2" on either side of the center point to secure the spear in position. Stitch from raw edge to raw edge crossing the center point to complete the block. Remove pins as you get to them. Stitch slowly and carefully. For the final pressing, pull a few stitches from the center seams so the allowances can be pressed circularly.

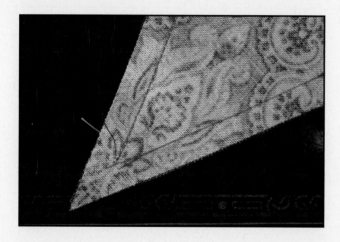

Despite all your care and precision, sometimes you will find a small gap or hole in the center when you are done. You can tighten it up by "draw-stringing" it using the same approach we learned when sewing seams with multiple intersections. Large holes usually need to be repaired by taking out the seams, finding out where the inaccuracies are and fixing them.

Make a small knot on your thread. Beginning at the base of one seam allowance, run your needle and thread precisely through the base of each seam allowance in the marked points. Proceed around the center of the block back to where you started, pulling the thread snug to gather all the points together. Backstitch, knot and finish

off the thread in the seam allowance rather than the sewing line.

· · · · · · · · · · ·
Mitered Seams

Mitering is a skill used in some block piecing and in border piecing as well. A mitered seam is a diagonal seam running from one inside corner to the outer corner. In a way, it is just another form of a set-in seam. It is easily done by hand as it requires point-to-point sewing, i.e., no sewing from raw edge to raw edge as is done with machine piecing. Look at the sample below. The Diamonds in the Window block is a simple clear example of the concept of mitering.

The red and black pieces must be attached to the pieced square but the final seam is the diagonal seam that connects them at the corner.

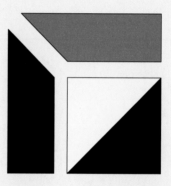

First sew the two pieces to the pieced square on adjacent sides, ignoring the diagonal seams. Sew precisely from corner to corner on each side as you would normally. If you are machine piecing, you need to make pencil marks 1/4" from the center corners in order to know where to stop and start in the center.

Now fold the center-pieced square in half on its diagonal, right sides together, so the diagonal seams of the red and black pieces are lying on top of each other. Match sewing lines (or mark back a diagonal sewing line on one side, if working by machine), pin, and sew the diagonal line connecting them. Your miter is complete.

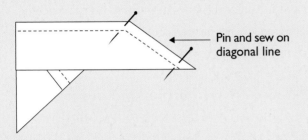

Pin and sew on diagonal line

Integrated Piecing: Mixing it All Up

Most quilt makers look at hand piecing and machine piecing as separate, stand-alone processes that don't play well with each other. When we think of using templates, we immediately picture traditional hand piecing to go with it. When patterns instruct rotary cutting, we automatically think of sewing machines.

Why? What if I told you it is perfectly possible to mix it all up and hand stitch rotary-cut pieces and machine piece template-cut pieces and also to mix all those techniques within one project?

In addition, there are some wonderful new methods developed for rotary cutting and machine piecing that can be adapted for handwork. Did you know that it is possible to sew quick triangles by hand? It is also possible to make folded corners by hand and chain sew. You can also sew machine pieced strip unit segments together by hand if you wish. I'll bet with time you will come up with other adaptations as well. It all contributes to total versatility in the ability to take your work with you.

Below are some ideas and strategies to help you plan for all eventualities and enable you to mix all your skills together. Only you can determine what you have in mind for each project and how you want to handle it. The best part is you can integrate it all and be totally portable!

Mixing Templates and Hand Piecing with Machine Piecing

Quilt makers have been machine sewing template-cut shapes since the invention of the sewing machine. The most basic adaptation to the machine stays exactly the same as described in the chapter on Hand Piecing on p. 7 with one exception. Match and pin sewing lines as usual, but when you get to the stitching, use an electric needle instead of a hand-held needle. That's simple enough, isn't it?

But you can avoid the use of pins if, when you are cutting your template-marked pieces, you cut a measured 1/4" seam allowance instead of estimating one. There are two ways to do this. See Cutting the Fabric on page 18 for more in-depth information.

The first way is to mark a cutting line by measuring and drawing 1/4" from the sewing line with a ruler. Cut the pieces out on this measured line.

The second way is to use a rotary cutter to cut the pieces directly from your fabric. It is helpful to mark your pieces on your fabric in nice neat rows from selvage to selvage almost in the form of strips. Then you can first cut long strips and crosscut the pieces from each strip.

There is another way to combine templates, hand piecing and machine piecing all together in one project. This is a method you would use when you do not have access to your rotary equipment; for example, if you are traveling (or otherwise away from your 'stuff') and want to start cutting and sewing your pieces by hand with the intention of machine piecing later when you have the chance. In this case, mark your fabric and then estimate oversize seam allowances when cutting out your pieces. Do not wildly over size them though as that will waste fabric. Hand piece while you can, and then later when you are back with your machine and rotary equipment, you can rotary cut the seams to a precise 1/4" as needed. This will enable you to machine piece as normal, aligning raw edges, without using pins to match sewing lines. It gives you access to the best of both worlds.

This is what I prefer to do most of the time when I think I may want to mix methods. The result is that I am set up to hand piece as much as I want, but if I have the opportunity or need to switch to machine piecing, I am ready to do so with minimal additional work. I only rotary cut the seam allowances I need as I go. Who knows, I may want to stop, grab it all up and head back out the door for more hand piecing.

Meanwhile, as I sew blocks by hand, I trim down my interior seams with scissors as soon as they are sewn. I do not trim down any seams that will fall on the outside edges of the block. Since I usually, but not always, machine piece my blocks to each other as well as sashes and borders, I can trim the outside edges of my completed blocks with the rotary cutter to precisely 1/4" from the sewing line. They are then ready to integrate with my rotary cut sashes and borders or any machine pieced blocks I have made. It keeps me versatile.

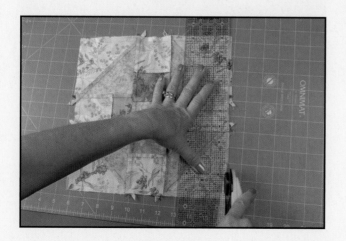

Hand Stitching Rotary Cut Pieces

I'll bet you thought you couldn't do this—but why not? I am currently working on a project that mixes templates and rotary cut elements in a fairly complex pattern. I take it with me everywhere and enjoy working on it in the evenings while I'm with my family or outside on a beautiful day. Rainy days find me at the machine.

When you set out to hand piece rotary cut squares and other units, you'll notice there is one thing missing—a marked sewing line. So, needing to know where to sew, why not just mark back a sewing line 1/4" from the raw edge of the rotary cutting? That's exactly what to do but there is an important concept you need to understand in order to do it properly.

It is important to mark with the 1/4" ruler line running on the perimeter of the fabric not on the edge. This is because a sewing pencil line has a dimension, a thickness. We do not want that dimension or thickness coming out of what will be the finished area of the piece. Therefore, the ruler line must lie outside the fabric edge so the marked pencil line is not too far in and falling inside the finished area of the piece.

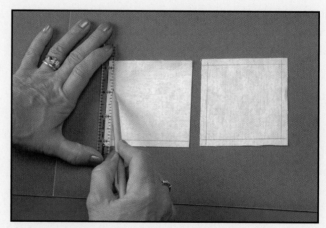

Here are a few other tips to keep in mind when marking back sewing lines:

1. Do not mark back a sewing line on all sides of each piece. Mark only the seam you plan to sew at that moment.

2. Do not mark a sewing line on both pieces to be sewn. Since you can accurately line up raw edges, you only need a sewing line on one side. Choose

to mark the side on which the line will be most visible, i.e., the lighter side.

3. Use a skinny ruler with clear 1/4" lines. They are more portable and easier to manipulate. Keep a small sandpaper board in your travel kit also.

4. Use a fine-line mechanical pencil for your markings as always.

The practice of marking back sewing lines goes hand-in-hand with the following skills adapted from rotary cutting and machine piecing. You'll find you will get pretty zippy at this marking-back skill with just a little practice.

Quick Triangles by Hand

You learned about Quick Triangles on p. 25 using rotary cutting and machine piecing skills. It's a simple little process that adapts easily to hand piecing as well.

Follow the same procedure as described on p. 25 in every way but instead of machine sewing on the lines, hand stitch. It's that simple. When you reach the end of one side, backstitch and knot but do not cut your thread. Instead, rotate your piece and begin stitching the second line by starting with a backstitch and loop knot and continuing on your way across the second seam. Finish off with a backstitch and knot as you would normally when hand piecing. Cut the square in half through the diagonal and press the triangles just as with the machine version.

If continuing on with hand piecing, you can mark back sewing lines on the pressed triangle units as needed or, alternately, return to machine piecing.

Folded Corners by Hand

Just as with Quick Triangles, folded corners can be made by hand as well. The procedure is exactly the same as the rotary-cut version of Folded Corners on p. 25 with one exception. Again, instead of using a sewing machine to stitch, you hand sew on the diagonal lines.

Continue assembling your block, as you prefer, either by hand with marked back sewing lines or by machine.

Chain Sewing By Hand

Yes, you can. There is no reason why you cannot chain sew by hand just as you do by machine. In fact, it is quite nice not having to stop every seam with a new knot when piecing by hand. Instead, once you are at the end of a seam, stop with a normal backstitch and loop knot. Do not clip the thread. Pick up the next seam to be sewn, take a stitch, pulling the thread almost all the way through, start the next seam with a backstitch and loop knot and continue on. There is no need to make a new quilters knot on the end of a thread to start a new seam. Once you are done with a string of sewing, clip the thread between the pieces. The process is exactly the same as when chain sewing by machine.

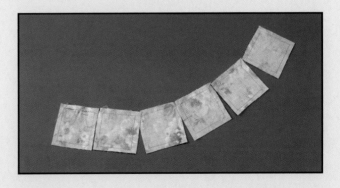

Sewing Strip Unit Segments by Hand

I'm sure by now you have realized there is no reason you can't hand piece your machine pieced and rotary cut segments. Align the raw edges, pin to secure and hand piece leaving free-standing seam allowances. I'm sure you would prefer to machine piece those segments but if your time dictates that you can't, why not take them with you and hand piece them until you are back at the machine?

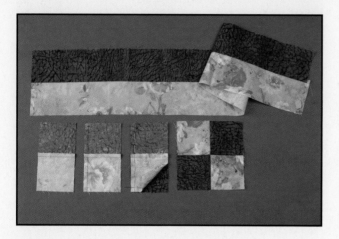

Finishing Your Quilt Top

O nce your blocks are complete, be sure to trim any oversize seam allowances on the perimeter of the blocks back to 1/4". Use the sewing lines as your guide. If you plan to continue on hand piecing, this will tidy up the edges. If you are planning to machine piece the rest of your top, this provides you with an accurate 1/4" seam with which to align any sashes or borders.

Cutting Sashes and Borders

For Hand-piecing

Most of us who hand piece our blocks still rotary cut and machine piece the big, long and boring-to-sew sashes and borders. I will sew pieced sashes and borders by hand but I make the big plain things by machine. Still, if you are a die-hard hand-piecer, or do not own rotary equipment, you can mark and cut your big sashes and borders in one of two ways.

The first is to rotary cut all the big pieces and mark back sewing lines if you find you want to hand piece them.

The second method is for those who do not own

rotary equipment or do not have it handy. You can mark directly on your fabric without making templates. The trick is to use your quilter's ruler as the template instead.

For example, if you want to mark and cut 2" x 12" sashing strips, press and lay your fabric out selvage to selvage. Place your ruler on the fabric with the desired 2" x 12" dimensions inside the raw edges of the fabric, aligning the ruler edges with straight grain as usual. Mark the right side and top of the ruler 2" across the top and 12" down the side.

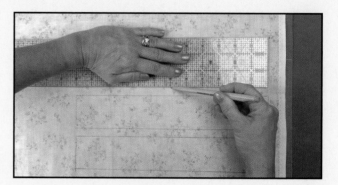

Continue up the length of the fabric marking the first two sides of the sashes as many times as will fit, while leaving room for seam allowances. Once done, turn the fabric around and place the 2" x 12" marks of the ruler on the lines you have already marked, and mark the last two sides. Continue working up the fabric, marking the last 2 sides of each sash. Continue in this fashion marking rows of sashes until you have the number you need and then cut them out 1/4" away from the marked sewing lines.

Use the same process to mark long strips for the borders. Pin and stitch sashes and borders in place as with any hand piecing.

For Machine piecing

Rotary cut sashes and borders are the norm for machine piecing although if you really wanted, you could mark and cut finished size pieces as in the section before, pin and machine stitch the strips in place. I think most of us would prefer to rotary cut, though.

Rotary cut strips are easily sewn to hand pieced blocks as long as you have left slightly oversized seams on the perimeter of your blocks and trimmed them to a precise 1/4" seam allowance. See p. 31 on Mixing Templates and Hand Piecing with Machine Piecing. Align raw edges as with basic machine piecing and sew.

Plain Borders

In this book, patterns are written for rotary cutting the big pieces. You will have to adjust your cutting if you choose do otherwise. I cut and sew border strips in a way to maximize fabric usage and eliminate waste. I also like the fact that with the method below the seams joining the border strips together fall randomly on the sides of the quilt, which will be less visible to the roving eye.

Read the instructions below. If you prefer a different method that uses more fabric, I advise you to adjust the yardage requirements accordingly. Be sure to trim the edges of your quilt top even before sewing borders in place.

1. Cut the number of strips indicated by the pattern.

2. Sew them end-to-end to make one very long border strip. I sew the strips together with a diagonal seam when I think the seam would be very visible on a plainer type of print. Some busy or directional prints do not require a diagonal seam and therefore it's a waste of time. In other cases, the borders are close in length to the 42" width of the fabric. In that case, I cut one strip in half and begin the stripping with a half strip and end it with the other half strip. This way, there will not be a seam close to the end of the border on the side of the quilt. Only you can discern these distinctions and decide what to do in individual cases.

To make a diagonal seam, lay the ends of the border strips right sides together as in the diagram. Draw a diagonal line from intersecting corner to intersecting corner as shown. Pin lightly.

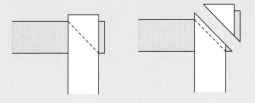

Stitch on the line. Fold the one strip over so it is straight to make sure it aligns properly. Cut the excess away from behind the strips 1/4" from the seam. Press. Repeat for each connection. Be sure to use thread that matches your fabric so you can press the seams open to make it less visible.

3. Measure the quilt through the center. Cut two strips this length from the long border strip. If you need to adjust where you make your cut so a diagonal seam does not fall directly at one end of the seam, do so. Sew the borders to the sides of the quilt top, matching half and quarter points between the border and the top. Ease any fullness evenly between these markers. Press away from the center of the quilt.

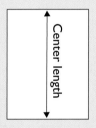

4. Measure through the center width of the quilt including the attached borders. Cut the last two border strips to this length, adjusting for the location of the diagonal seam if necessary. Sew the borders to the top and bottom of the quilt. Press away from the center of the quilt.

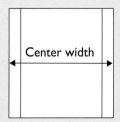

Completing Your Quilt

Once your quilt top is done, it will be ready to layer, baste and quilt either by hand or machine. There are many books available that deal with these subjects in depth. I recommend you use one of them for more information on those subjects.

Binding Your Quilt

Binding yardages for the patterns in this book are based on cutting 2 1/4" strips from selvage to selvage to make a double-fold binding. Bindings should be the length of the four sides of the quilt plus about 10"-12" for turning and finishing the ends. If you prefer another method of binding construction, you may need to adjust the binding yardage accordingly.

1. Sew the strips together using a diagonal seam in the same fashion as described in the previous section on borders. Press the seams open. The diagonal open seams will disperse nicely across the binding resulting in reduced bulk.

2. Press the strips in half lengthwise, wrong sides together.

3. Trim the batting and backing of your quilt even with the top and square off the corners of the quilt.

4. In the center of one edge of the quilt, align the raw edges of the binding with the raw edges of the quilt top. Leaving about 6" free as a starting tail, sew the binding to the edge of the quilt with a 1/4"-wide seam allowance. Stop stitching 1/4" from the corner of the first side. Backstitch and remove the quilt from the machine.

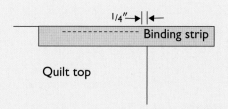

5. At the corner, flip the binding straight up from the corner so it forms a continuous line with the adjacent side of the quilt top.

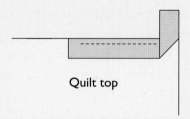

6. Fold the binding straight down so it lies on the top of the next side. Pin the pleat in place that is formed here. Starting at the edge, stitch the second side of the binding to the quilt, stopping 1/4" from the next corner. Repeat this process for the remaining corners.

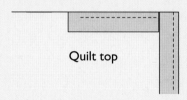

7. When you have turned the last corner and are nearing the point where you began, stop and overlap the loose binding tails. Trim the starting tail to a 45° angle that goes in the same direction as the binding seams. Trim the ending tail at the same angle and to a length that fits completely in the angled fold of the starting tail without a lot of overlap. Tuck the ending tail into the starting tail. Pin both tails in place securing the layers and finish the seam.

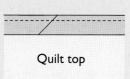

Quilt top

8. With a matching thread, slipstitch the diagonal fold of the starting tail to the ending tail so it looks like a regular seam. Roll the binding to the back of the quilt and slip stitch it on the back with matching thread, folding the corners into a miter.

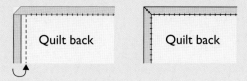

Quilt back   Quilt back

. . . .

Labeling Your Quilt

Once quilted and bound, be sure to sign and date your quilt. Labels can be simple or elaborate. Include your name, the date, city, state and the name of the quilt. If it is a gift, you may want to add the recipient's name and the occasion or any other interesting information about the quilt for future generations.

The Quilts and Projects

There are 14 patterns in this section. Many have multiple samples showing variations in color or design to inspire you and get your creative juices flowing. Instructions are given for one sample with notes, when feasible, on how to adapt to the other variations. I strongly encourage you to read the instructional sections of this book so you understand the principles involved.

If you would like to preview a pattern by making just one block, you can do so. Most of the assembly instructions are written for one block at a time. If you read through those instructions, you can discern how many pieces you need to cut to make just one practice block before deciding to cut the entire quilt.

Templates are provided for all projects with one or two exceptions. Remember that if you are hand piecing, use the finished size templates. If machine piecing, you may opt to use either the finished size templates or the templates with seam allowances included although I always prefer finished size markings with measured and cut 1/4" seam allowances.

You will also find that for some projects alternate rotary cutting instructions are given for geometric shapes. This information is provided for several reasons; 1) if you prefer, you can rotary cut and hand piece with marked-back sewing lines, 2) if you are planning to mix hand and machine piecing, you can move back and forth between the two with ease, and 3) if you prefer to machine piece the entire project, you can do so without using all templates. Rotary cutting instructions are given for all borders, setting pieces, and sashing strips. If you plan to hand piece these big pieces, please see p. 35 on Cutting Sashes and Borders for more detailed information.

As always, cut the largest pieces first, whether template or rotary cut. You can always get smaller pieces out of leftovers but not large pieces.

In some of the rotary cutting instructions, you will see two shortcut symbols. The first ▱ indicates to cut squares in half once diagonally to produce half-square triangles. The second symbol ⊠ indicates to cut squares in half on both diagonals to produce quarter-square triangles.

Arrows in the assembly diagrams indicate where to press seams at each point in the construction process. Generally, if you are hand piecing you will not press until the block is complete although gentle finger pressing along the way makes the final job of pressing a little clearer and easier. Use these arrows as a guide for finger pressing. If you are machine piecing, these arrows are essential in ensuring that the seams butt and the blocks lay flat when done.

If necessary, with each project, there will be a referral list of sections in the book to turn to for the skills required beyond the basics to complete that project. Although it is assumed you have read the skills sections of this book before attempting any projects, be sure to take a moment to refresh your memory by reviewing those specific sections listed before starting each project.

And finally, 1-3 thread spools indicate the difficulty level of each project with 1 spool being the easiest. These are geared towards hand piecing skills only. You may be surprised to find some blocks you thought were difficult are not as challenging when pieced by hand as they would be by machine.

Piece in the Garden

Piece in the Garden

Quilt Size: 28" x 52"

*Hand and machine pieced by
Donna Lynn Thomas, Basehor, KS,
hand quilted by Donna Thomas
and Denise Mariano, Lansing, KS,
2006*

I hand pieced the flower blocks
and center of this quilt as well
as hand appliquéd the vines and
leaves. Once assembled, the eight
pieced pansy, lily and honeysuckle
blocks composing the center of the
quilt are accented with appliquéd
vines and leaves for a lovely finish.
I machine pieced the checkerboard
border although there is no reason
the border could not be hand-
pieced as well. It is also entirely
feasible to strip piece, rotary cut
segments, and then hand stitch
the segments into four-patch units
if you wish. The choices are yours.
Pattern provided.

Nighttime Garden Glow

Quilt Size: 20" x 44"
Hand and machine pieced by Donna Lynn Thomas, Basehor, KS, machine quilted by Freda Smith, Kansas City, KS 2007

The bright prints used for the flower blocks just glow against the black background fabric. Once the checkerboard border was in place, the quilt did not call for more borders so I stopped right there. The pot fabric was a piece of hand-painted marble I had found many years ago. It was exciting to find just the right use for it.

Festival of Flowers

Quilt size: 28" x 52"
*Hand and machine pieced
and machine quilted by
Linda Harker, Kansas City,
KS, 2007*

Beautiful bright colors
bring spring to mind
with this rendition of
the same pattern. Linda
says she had forgotten
how much she truly
enjoyed hand piecing
and is looking forward to
doing a lot more in the
future. She noted how she
could take it anywhere
and wasn't limited to
appliqué projects for travel
anymore.

Lily

Block size: 4 7/8" finished size
Number of blocks: 3

Honeysuckle

Block Size: 5" finished size
Number of blocks: 2

Pansy

Block size: 5" finished size
Number of blocks: 3

Fabric Requirements:

- ◈ 5/8 yd. blue floral print for outer border
- ◈ 3/8 yd. pink print for checkerboard border
- ◈ 11/2 yds. cream print
- ◈ 1/2 yd. green print for stem and vines
- ◈ 1 fat quarter brown print for flower pot
- ◈ 9" x 20" pieces of assorted greens for block piecing and appliqué leaves
- ◈ 9" squares of dark blue, medium blue, dark pink, medium pink, dark lilac and medium lilac for block piecing
- ◈ 1 5/8 yd. for backing
- ◈ 3/8 yd. for binding

Note: You will also need appliqué supplies to include needles and thread to match the green prints for vines, leaves and stems.

Cutting Instructions:

Cutting instructions are given separately for each block and the flower pot and then in total for completing the rest of the quilt.

Refer to special cutting skills on:

- ◈ Template Construction on p. 8

Pansy block

From the medium blue, cut:

- ◈ 12 Template C

From the dark blue, cut:

- ◈ 6 Template C
- ◈ 3 Template D

From the dark green, cut:

- ◈ 6 Template C
- ◈ 3 Template D

From the medium green, cut:

- ◈ 3 Template B
- ◈ 3 Template B-R

From the cream print, cut:

- ◈ 18 Template C
- ◈ 6 Template D
- ◈ 3 Template A
- ◈ 3 Template A-R

Lily block

From the medium pink, cut:

- ◈ 6 Template E

From the dark pink, cut:

- ◈ 6 Template E

From the green print, cut:

- ◈ 3 Template H

From the cream print, cut:
- ◆ 3 Template F
- ◆ 6 Template G

Honeysuckle block

From the dark lilac, cut:
- ◆ 2 Template K
- ◆ 2 Template K-R

From the medium lilac, cut:
- ◆ 2 Template J

From the cream print, cut:
- ◆ 4 Template M
- ◆ 4 Template N

Flower Pot

From the brown print, cut:
- ◆ 1 Template O for the flower pot
- ◆ 1 Template Q for the flower pot stand
- ◆ 1 Template T for the flower pot base

From the cream print, cut:
- ◆ 1 Template P
- ◆ 1 Template P-R
- ◆ 2 Template R
- ◆ 1 Template S
- ◆ 1 Template S-R
- ◆ 1 Template V

Cutting to complete the quilt top:

Be very careful to measure and cut accurately when cutting the pieces from the cream print. There are many pieces with similar or close dimensions that could easily be confused. It is a good idea to label and pin the assorted pieces with their dimensions as you cut them.

From the cream print, cut:

1-8 1/2" x 42" strip, cross cut into the following pieces:
- ◆ 2 - 4 1/2" x 8 1/2" pieces
- ◆ 1 - 3 5/8" x 8 1/2" piece
- ◆ 2 - 3 1/2" x 8 1/2" pieces
- ◆ 5 - 2 1/2" x 8 1/2" pieces
- ◆ 2 - 1 5/8" x 8 1/2" pieces
- ◆ 3 - 1 1/2" x 8 1/2" pieces

1 - 5 1/2" x 42" strip, crosscut into the following pieces:
- ◆ 5 - 2 1/2" x 5 1/2" pieces
- ◆ 5 - 1 1/2" x 5 1/2" pieces
- ◆ 3 - 2 5/8" x 5 3/8" pieces
- ◆ 3 - 1 1/2" x 5 3/8" pieces

120 Template Y OR 5 - 1 1/2" x 42" strips for the checkerboard border

From the green print for the stem and vines, cut:
- ◆ 1 - 14" square for bias vines
- ◆ 1 - 1 1/4" x 25" strip for the center stem

From the assorted green prints for leaves, cut:
- ◆ 9 Template X (marked on the right side for appliqué)
- ◆ 10 Template W (marked on the right side for appliqué)

From the pink print, cut:
- ◆ 120 Template Y OR 5 - 1 1/2" x 42" strips for the checkerboard border

From the blue floral print, cut:
- ◆ 5- 4 1/2" x 42" strips for the outer border

Assembly Instructions:

Instructions are given individually for each block and the pot and then for the rest of the quilt as a whole.

Pansy Block

1. Sew a green triangle to a cream triangle and a dark blue triangle to a cream triangle. Make 2 of each.

2. Sew a medium triangle to a cream Template A and a Template AR as shown. Make 1 of each.

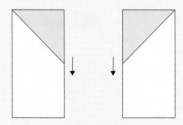

3. Sew a medium blue triangle and a cream triangle to opposite sides of a Template B and BR as shown. Make 1 of each,

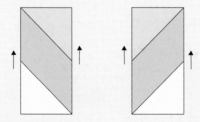

4. Using the pieced units from the steps above as well as the 2 cream, 1 dark blue, and 1 green square, assemble the pansy block as shown. If you have pressed as indicated by the arrows, your diagonal seams should butt when matching. Repeat steps 1-4 to complete a total of 3 Pansy blocks.

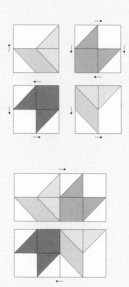

Lily Block

Refer to special skills sections on:

◈ Set in Seams on p. 27.

1. Sew 2 medium pink diamonds together as shown. Sew a dark pink diamond to either side of the pair to make a Lily.

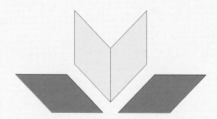

2. Set-in two cream triangles and a cream square as shown. Sew a green triangle to the bottom of the Lily to complete the block. Repeat steps 1-2 to make 2 more Lily blocks.

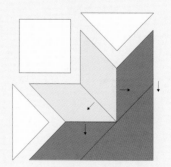

Honeysuckle Block

Refer to special skills sections on:

◈ Curved Seams on p. 28.

◈ Set-in Seams on p. 27.

1. Sew 2 dark lilac, 1 medium lilac and 1 green unit together as shown to make a honeysuckle flower.

2. Sew the cream side units in place as shown with curved seams and set-in seams. Repeats Steps 1 and 2 to make another Honeysuckle block.

Flower Pot

1. Sew a cream P and PR to either side of the brown pot as shown.

2. Sew a cream R to either side of the brown pot stand.

3. Sew a cream S and SR to either side of the pot base as shown.

4. Sew the units from Steps 1-3 together as shown. Sew the cream Template V to the bottom of the pot to complete the Flower Pot Block.

5. Sew the 2 cream 4 1/2" x 8 1/2" pieces to each side of the pot to finish the pot base.

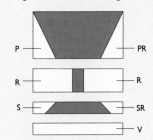

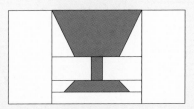

Make a pot base

Quilt Center Assembly

1. Using the diagram layout as a guide, sew the 2 Honeysuckle blocks, 2 Lily blocks, and 2 Pansy blocks intro 2 columns as shown. Be very careful to use the size pieces indicated, as some are close in dimensions. If in doubt, remeasure what you have to confirm sizes. Also pay close attention to the up and down orientation of the flowers, referring to the quilt photo as a guide.

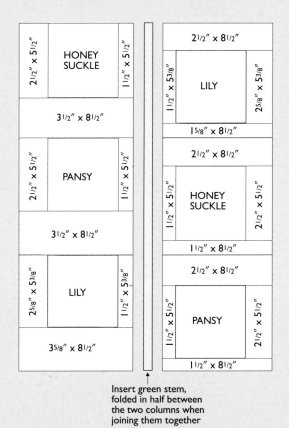

Insert green stem, folded in half between the two columns when joining them together

2. Press the 1 1/4" x 25" green stem in half wrong sides together along its length. Pin it to the center seam of the left column. It is slightly longer than the column.

3. Place the right column over the stem and left column. Stitch the 2 columns and the stem together to make the main body of the quilt center. Trim the stem to be even with the flower columns. The stem will be appliquéd to the right column later. For now leave it unsecured.

4. Sew a Lily block and a Pansy block together with the remaining cream pieces as indicated in the diagram below to make the flower top.

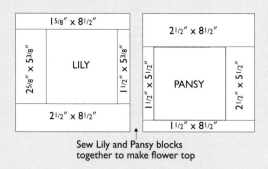

Sew Lily and Pansy blocks together to make flower top

5. Sew the Flower top and the Flower Pot to the top and bottom of the flower columns as shown.

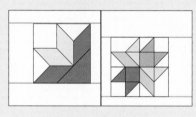

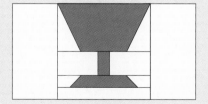

6. Cut the 14" green square in half on its diagonal. Then cut 1" strips from either side of the diagonal cut to create bias strips. Cut 5-6 lengths of bias strips.

Cut 1" bias strips

7. Carefully press the bias strips in half on their lengths with wrong sides together avoiding stretching them with aggressive pressing. Measuring from the fold, baste the strip 1/4" along its length. If working by hand, use a ruler to draw a chalk line 1/4" from the fold. Loosely stitch on this line. Trim the raw edges to 1/8" from the basting line. Trim the tails straight.

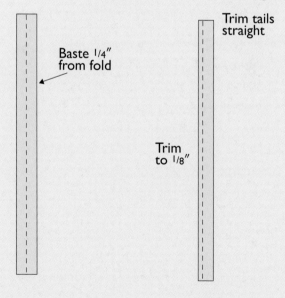

Trim tails straight

Baste 1/4" from fold

Trim to 1/8"

8. Turn under and baste the edges of the appliqué leaves along the marked chalk lines.

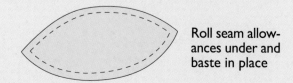

Roll seam allowances under and baste in place

9. Using the quilt photo as a guide, lay out the stems on the quilt center meandering among the blocks in a pleasing arrangement. I tried to make sure a vine came near the green end point of each block and tucked the raw edges of the vines under the loose center stalk. I covered the stalk end with vines. I followed no set pattern but just played with it as I went. Once I was pleased with the vine arrangements, I pinned them in place with small appliqué pins. Some people prefer to replace the pins with thread basting.

10. Place the leaves on the quilt in a pleasing arrangement, referring to the photo if necessary. Be sure to cover the vine end on the pot with a cluster of leaves and the vine and stalk grouping at the top with a leaf or two also. If you want more leaves, cut and add some more. If not, take some away. Once the leaves are placed where you want them, secure them in place with pins only so that you can fold them out of the way when you sew the vines in place.

11. Begin appliquéing the vines in place first. I preferred to stitch the folded edge of the vines first. Use matching thread. Then stitch the other side of the vines by folding the raw edges under the stem and appliquéing the newly created fold down. Be sure to turn the raw edges under far enough so that the basting does not show. If you need to trim more of the raw edge away, do so. This method gives a nice three-dimensional look to the vines. As I worked my way up the quilt, I also stitched the loose green stalk down. It cannot be secured until the vines that slip under it are appliquéd first.

12. Appliqué the leaves in place. Make sure you have the leaves positioned as you want them. If you wish to replace the pin basting with thread, now is the time. Using a thread color to match each leaf print, stitch the leaves in place to complete the center of the quilt.

Quilt Top Assembly

1. If you plan to strip piece the checkerboard border, sew the 5 - 1 1/2" x 42" cream and pink strips into 5 strip units as shown. Cut a total of 120 segments from the strip units. Cut them 1 1/2" wide. If you are using templates skip to Step 3.

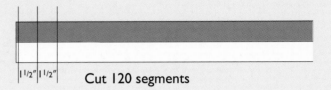

1 1/2" 1 1/2"   **Cut 120 segments**

2. Sew the segments into pairs to make 60 four-patch units. Skip to Step 4.

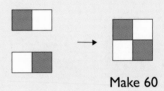

Make 60

3. If you are using template-cut pieces for the checkerboard border, sew 2 pink and 2 cream squares together to make a four-patch. Make 60.

4. Sew the four-patch units into 2 border strips of 20 four-patch units and 2 border strips of 10 four-patch units each. Please note the orientation of the four-patch units in each of the two lengths of borders. The orientation is important in order for the checkerboard effect to be created at the corners where the borders meet.

5. Measure the dimensions of your quilt top through the center length and width. It should measure 16 1/2" x 40 1/2" including seam allowances. If it is shorter than that you will have to take in miniscule amounts between your four-patch units at multiple points across the length of each border in order to make it fit. If the quilt measures more than it should, you will have to let out seams in small amounts across multiple

Make 2 for top and bottom

Make 2 for sides

places in the border. The small increment additions or deletions should go undetected in the end. One large take-in or let-out would stand out. Adjust the length of your side borders as necessary.

6. Sew the side borders in place. Now adjust the top and bottom borders as necessary following the same guidelines as above.

7. Following the general instructions on pp. 35 for Plain Borders, sew the blue floral border to the quilt top.

8. Layer, baste and quilt as desired.

9. Bind with 5 - 2 1/4"-wide cross-grain double fold binding strips.

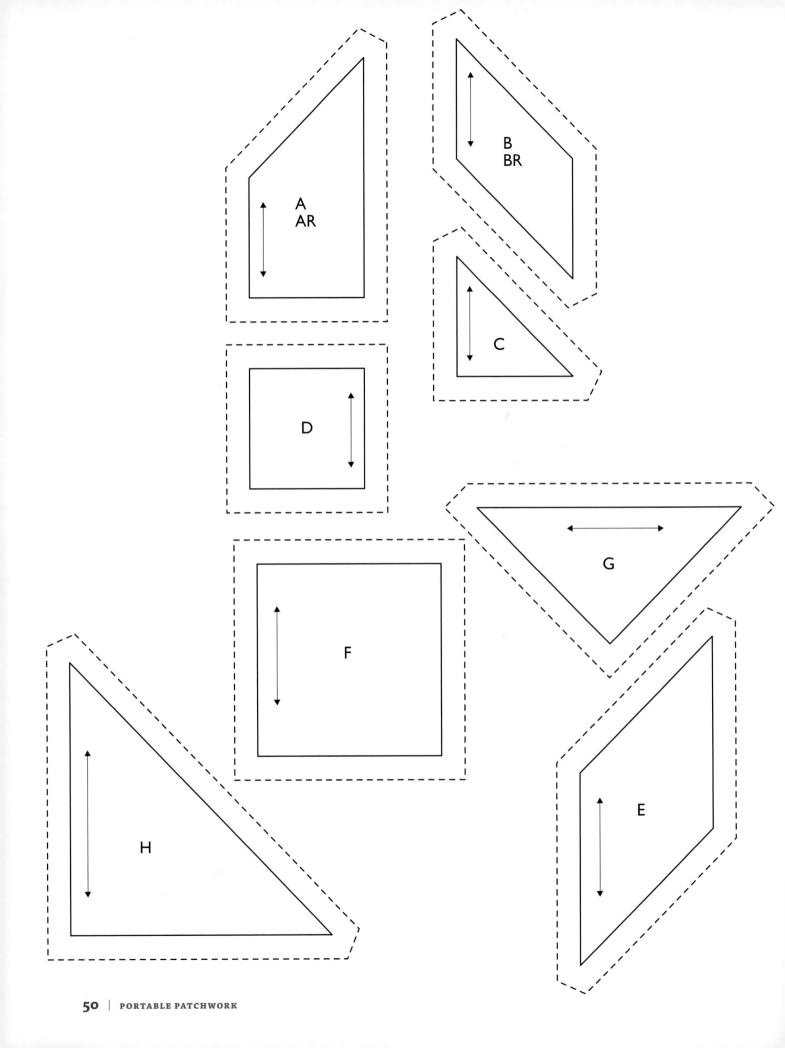

A
AR

B
BR

C

D

G

F

E

H

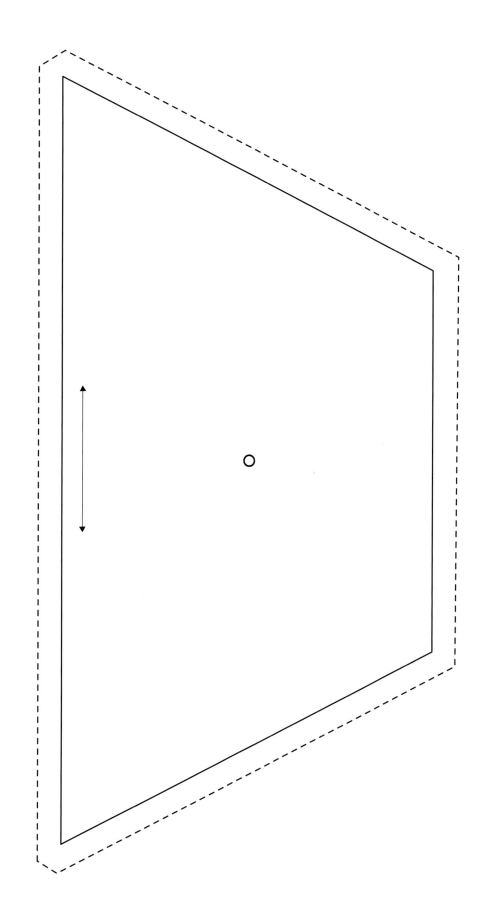

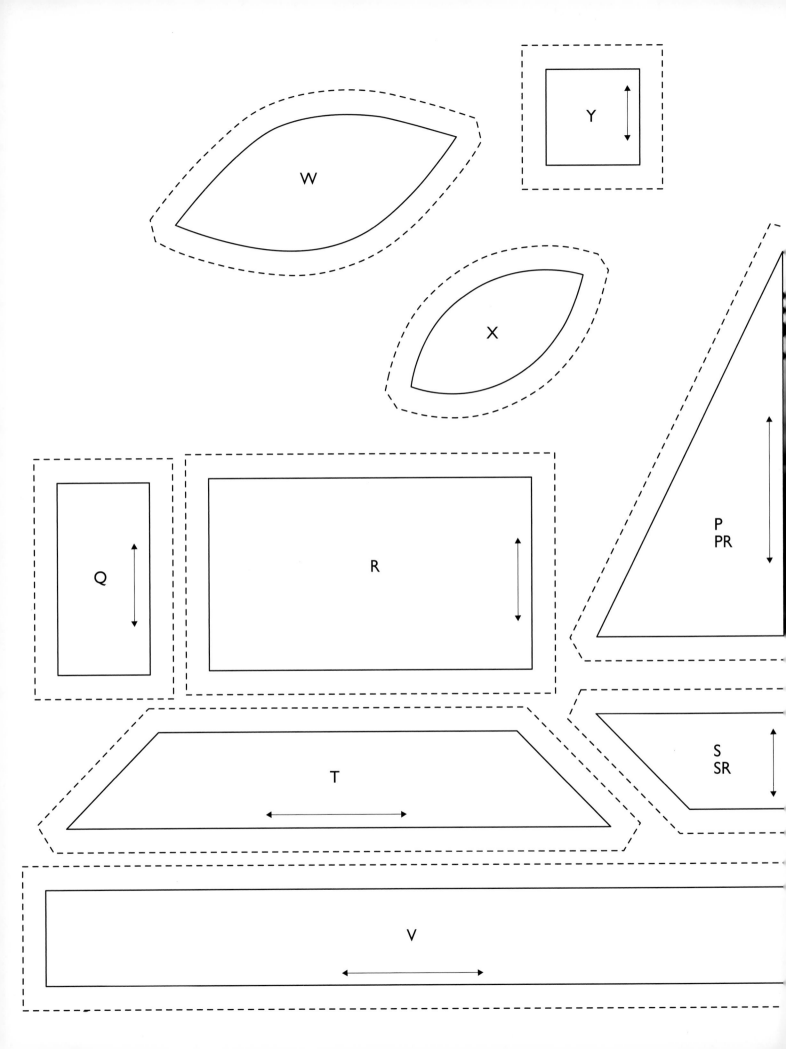

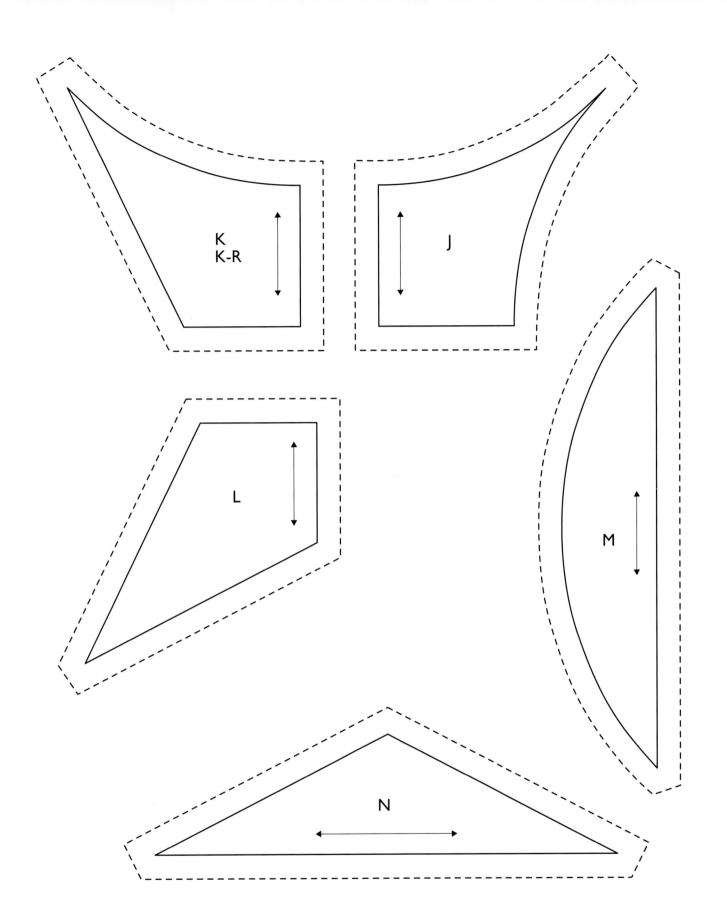

St. Louis Nosegay 🧵🧵🧵

St. Louis Nosegay

Quilt Size: 82" square

Hand and machine pieced by Donna Lynn Thomas, Basehor, KS, machine quilted by Sandy Gore, Liberty, MO 2006

Two blocks, St. Louis Star and Nosegay are set on point in this luscious, rich quilt. Together they create a circular motion in the center of the quilt. I used multiple dark greens and purple prints but you may wish to combine some of them and use fewer prints.

Nosegay

Block Size: 12"
Number of Blocks: 4

St. Louis Star

Block Size: 12"
Number of Blocks: 9

Fabric Requirements:

◈ 2 1/8 yd. medium green floral print for block piecing and outer border

◈ 5/8 yd. dark green #1 for St. Louis Star piecing

◈ 1/4 yd. dark green #2 for Nosegay piecing

◈ 1 1/4 yd. dark purple star print for both blocks and border #4

◈ 3/4 yd. medium purple print #1 for St. Louis Star piecing

◈ 1/2 yd. each of medium purple prints #2 and #3 for Nosegay piecing

◈ 1 3/4 yd. cream print for both blocks

◈ 1 yd. dark green #3 for borders

◈ 7/8 yd. purple plaid for setting triangles

◈ 1 yd. light plum print for pieced border

◈ 5/8 yd. for binding

◈ 5 yds. for backing

Cutting Instructions:

Note: These blocks have several reverse templates so be very careful and make sure you are marking the correct image. See p. 8 on Template Construction for more information.

From the medium green floral print, cut:

◈ 36 Template H for St. Louis Star piecing

◈ 16 Template F for Nosegay piecing

◈ 8 - 5 1/2" x 42" strips for the outer border

From dark green #1, cut:

◈ 36 Template H-R for St. Louis Star piecing

From dark green #2, cut:

◈ 16 Template A for Nosegay piecing

◈ 16 Template A-R for Nosegay piecing

From the dark purple star print, cut:

◈ 36 Template J for St. Louis Star piecing

◈ 16 Template A for Nosegay piecing

◈ 16 Template A-R for Nosegay piecing

◈ 8 - 2" x 42" strips for the 4th border

From the medium purple print #1, cut:

◈ 36 Template J-R for St. Louis Star piecing

◈ 12 - 4" squares, for the pieced border

From medium purple print #2, cut:

◈ 16 Template A for Nosegay piecing

◈ 12 - 4" squares, for the pieced border

From medium purple print #3, cut:

◈ 16 Template A-R for Nosegay piecing

◈ 12 - 4" squares, for the pieced border

From the cream print, cut:

◈ 36 Template H for St. Louis Star piecing

◈ 36 Template H-R for St. Louis Star piecing

- 16 Template G for Nosegay piecing (transfer the slash mark on the template to each piece to indicate the outside edge)
- 16 Template E for Nosegay piecing
- 16 Template D for Nosegay piecing
- 32 Template C for Nosegay piecing
- 16 Template B for Nosegay piecing

From the purple plaid, cut:
- 2 - 18 1/2" squares, cut ⊠ for side-set triangles
- 2 -10" squares, cut ◱ for corner triangles
- 12 - 4" squares for the pieced border

From the dark green #3, cut:
- 13 - 2 1/2" x 42" strips, for borders #1 and #3

From the light plum print, cut:
- 22 - 6 1/4" squares, cut ⊠ for the pieced borders
- 8 - 3 3/8" squares, cut ◱ for the pieced borders

Refer to special skills on:
- Set-in Seams on p. 26

St. Louis Star:

1. Sew a dark purple star J to a medium purple #1 J-R as shown. Make 4.

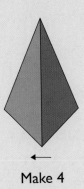

Make 4

2. Sew a green floral H to a cream H-R as shown. Make 4. Sew a dark green #1 H-R to a cream H as shown. Make 4. Be very careful, as it is easy to get these reverse pieces mixed up.

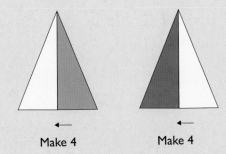

Make 4   Make 4

3. Sew a medium floral/cream unit to the dark purple side of a unit from Step 1. Sew a dark green/cream unit to the medium purple side of the same unit. Make 4 large pieced triangles.

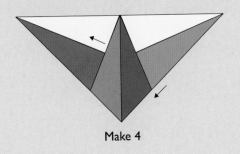

Make 4

4. Sew the 4 triangles together to complete a St. Louis Star block. Press seams in a counterclockwise direction. Repeat Steps 1-4 to make a total of 9 St. Louis Star blocks.

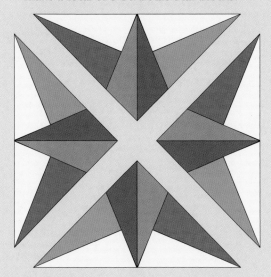

Nosegay:

1. Sew 4 medium floral F to 4 cream G as shown to make a block center. Be sure to place the edge of G with the slash mark on the outside as you piece.

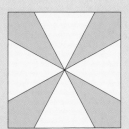

Make 4

2. Sew a dark green #2 A and A-R to either side of a cream E as shown. Make 4 leaf units. Sew the 4 leaf units to the block center as shown.

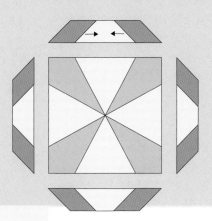

3. Sew a dark purple star A and A-R, a medium purple #2 A, and a medium purple #3 A-R together as shown. Make 4 purple flowers.

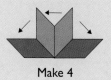

Make 4

4. Sew the purple flowers to the green leaves as shown.

5. Referring to Set-in Seams on p. 26 set in the 4 cream D, C, and B pieces as shown to complete a Nosegay block. Repeat Steps 1-6 to make a total of 4 Nosegay blocks.

Make one top and one bottom border

Quilt Assembly

1. Lay out the 9 St. Louis Star blocks, the 4 Nosegay blocks and the large purple plaid side-set and corner triangles as shown. Sew them into diagonal rows and join the rows together to complete the center of the quilt.

2. Following the general instructions on pp. 35 for Plain Borders, sew the 2 1/2" dark green inner border to the quilt top.

3. Lay out 11 assorted medium purple 4" squares, 20 light plum quarter-square triangles, and 4 light plum half-square triangles as shown. Sew them together to make a side border. Make 2 side borders. Measure them against the center length of the quilt top. If they are too long, take in tiny amounts on many seams to adjust the borders to the proper length. Once adjusted, sew them to the sides of the quilt top.

4. 4. Lay out 13 assorted medium purple 4" squares, 24 light plum quarter-square triangles, and 4 light plum half-square triangles as shown. Sew them together to make a long border. Make 2 for the top and bottom of the quilt. Measure them against the center width of the quilt top, including the side borders. If they are too long, take in tiny amounts on many seams to adjust the borders to the proper length. Once adjusted, sew them to the top and bottom of the quilt top.

5. Following the general instructions on pp. 35 for Plain Borders, sew the dark green, purple and green floral borders to the quilt top.

6. Layer, baste and quilt as desired.

7. Bind with 9 - 2 1/4"-wide cross-grain double fold binding strips.

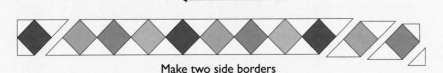

Make two side borders

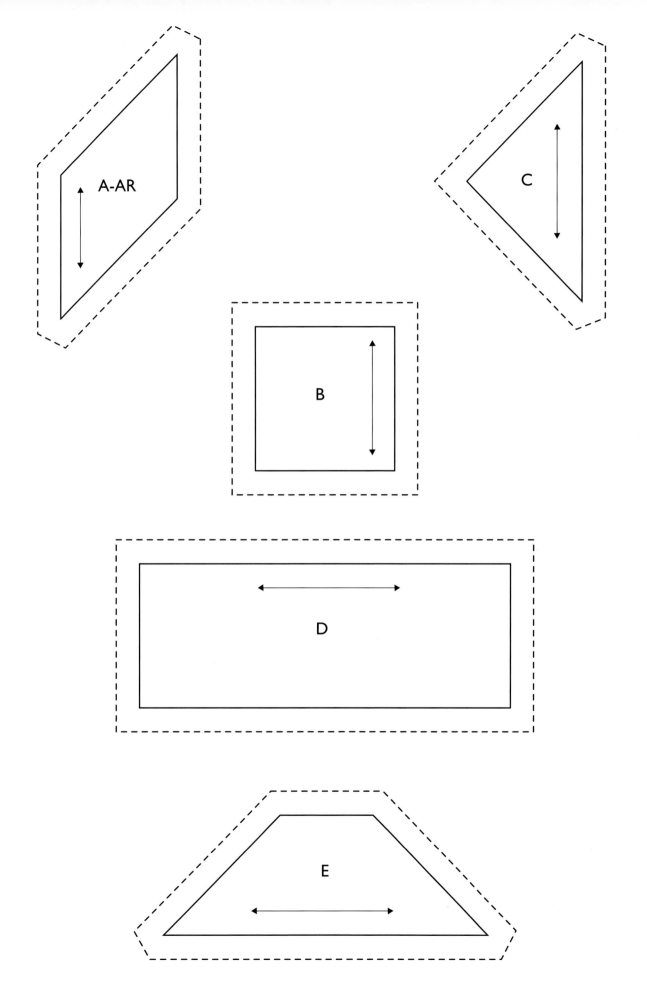

A-AR

C

B

D

E

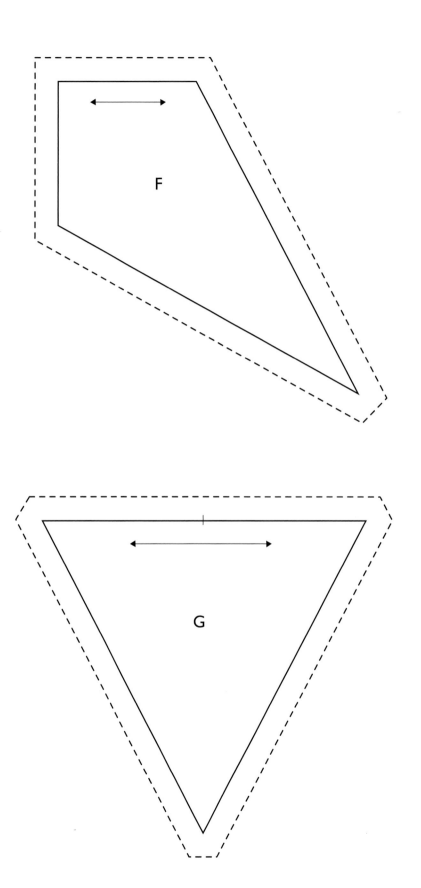

F

G

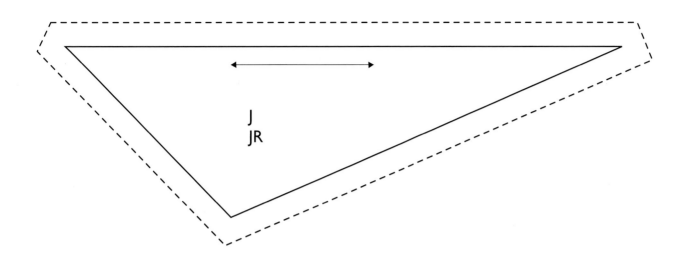

J
JR

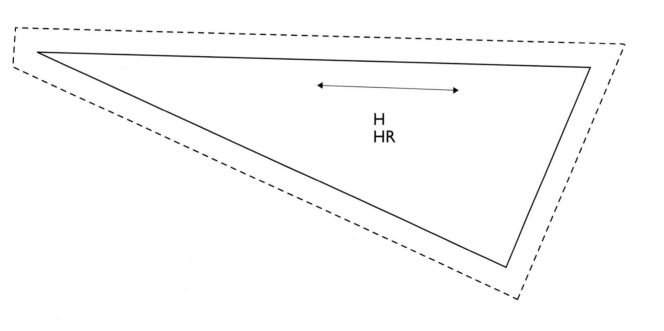

H
HR

Asian Pinwheels for Ann

Quilt size: 37" square

Designed and hand pieced by Ann Woodward, Collegeville, PA, hand quilted by her mother, Mary Louise Kulesza, Collegeville, PA, 2006

Ann, a long time quilting buddy and contributor to my previous books, had just finished hand piecing this top when I told her I was writing a new book on the same subject. She was so excited and e-mailed me that she would love to finish it for the book. The next day I learned she had unexpectedly passed away gently in her sleep at too young an age. Her mother Mary Louise, also an expert quilter, finished the quilt and sent it to me. The fabric choices were a new direction for Ann but still kept true to her soft and elegant look. It is a glorious finale to a too short life. Pattern provided.

Tribute to Ann

Quilt size: 40" square

Hand pieced by Donna Lynn Thomas, Basehor, KS, machine quilted by Freda Smith, Prairie Village, KS 2007

I loved the Pinwheel blocks Ann found and used in her quilt and just had to try my hand, so to speak, at them myself. A little different from the usual pinwheels we see, they were fun to piece and I enjoyed making these blocks as much as Ann did. Set together alternately, they create a nice overall design.

Block A

Asian Pinwheels for Ann

Block size: 10"

Number of blocks:
5 Block A,
4 Block B

Block B

Fabric Requirements:

- ◈ 1/2 yd. large floral print for block piecing
- ◈ 3/8 yd. plum print for block piecing
- ◈ 12" square turquoise print for block piecing
- ◈ 1 fat quarter or 1/4 yd. green print for block piecing
- ◈ 1 yd. cream print for block piecing and inner border
- ◈ 1/2 yd. lavender print for outer border
- ◈ 3/8 yd. for binding

Cutting Instructions:

Note: Templates B and E MUST be marked face down on the wrong side of the fabric. They are not symmetrical and therefore, direction matters. Also, when tracing Template E onto plastic, please transfer the slash marks on two of the seam allowances to the template edges. Then when marking the template on the wrong side of the fabric please make a pencil mark in those two seam allowances—these marks identify the two long sides of the parallelogram and will be necessary for matching later.

From the large floral print, cut:
- ◈ 20 Template F for Block A
- ◈ 16 Template B for Block B

From the plum print, cut:
- ◈ 20 Template E for Block A
- ◈ 16 Template A for Block B

From the turquoise print, cut:
- ◈ 16 Template C for Block B

From the green print, cut:
- ◈ 16 Template E for Block B

From the cream print, cut:
- ◈ 36 Template A for Blocks A and B
- ◈ 20 Template G for Block A
- ◈ 16 Template D for Block B
- ◈ 4 - 1 1/2" x 42" strips for the inner border

From the lavender print, cut:
- ◈ 4 - 3" x 42" strips for the outer border

Assembly Instructions:

Block A:

1. Sew a cream A and G to the top 2 sides of a plum E. Align the plum piece so that the long edge is sewn to A. Make 4 pieced triangles.

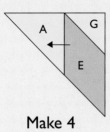

Make 4

2. Sew a floral F to each pieced triangle as shown. Make 4 pieced squares. Sew the pieced squares together to complete a Block A. Repeat steps 1 and 2 to make 4 more Block A.

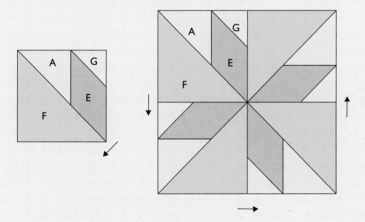

Block B:

1. Sew a cream A and D to either side of a floral B as shown. Make 4 pieced triangles.

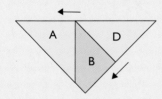

2. Sew a turquoise C and a green E to either side of a plum A as shown. Align the long edge of the E with the A unit. Make 4 pieced strips.

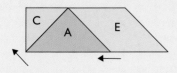

3. Sew a pieced strip to a pieced triangle from Step 1 as shown. Make 4 quarter-block pieced triangles.

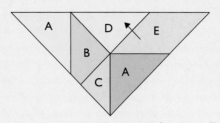

4. Sew the 4 quarter-blocks together to complete a Block B. Repeat Steps 1-4 to make 3 more Block B.

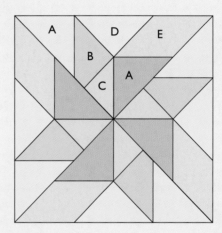

Finishing the Top

1. Lay out the 5 Block A and 4 Block B as shown in the photo. If you have pressed as directed, all seams should butt when matching. Sew the blocks into rows and join the rows together to complete the quilt center.

2. Following the general directions on p. 35 for Plain Borders, sew the cream borders to the quilt followed by the lavender borders.

3. Layer, baste and quilt as desired.

4. Bind with 4 - 2 1/4"-wide cross-grain double fold binding strips.

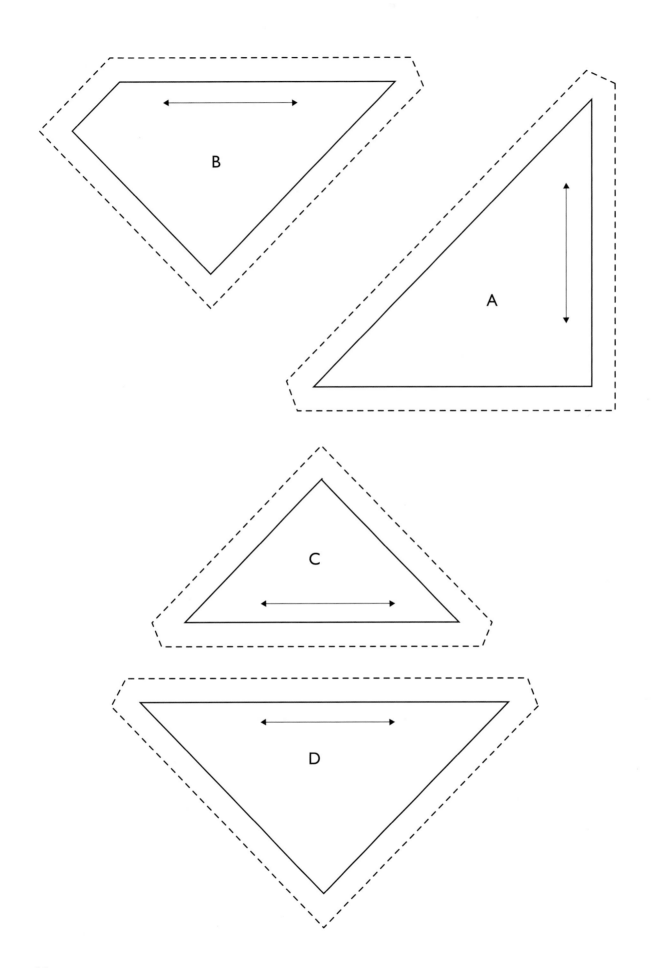

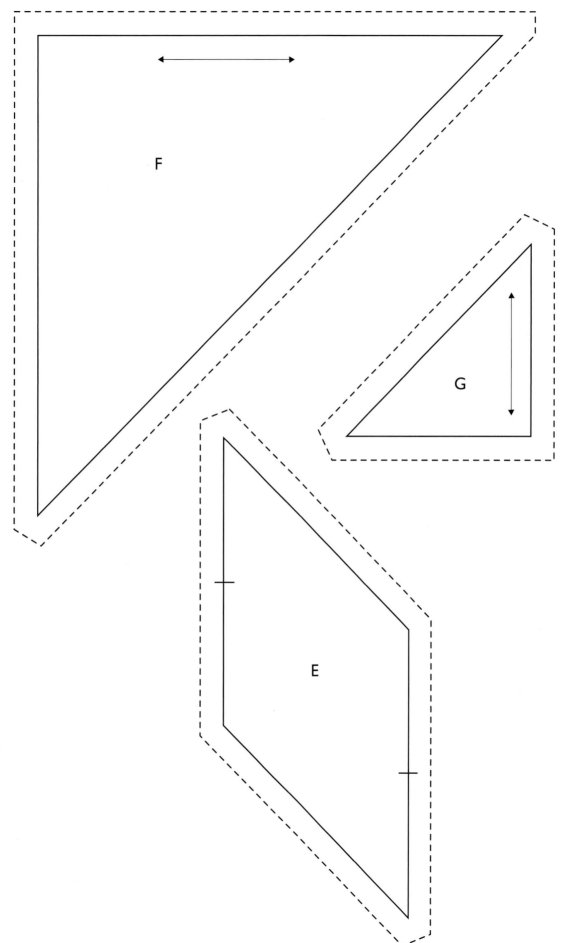

F

G

E

Missouri Riverboat Paddles

Quilt size: 52 1/4" x 52 1/4"
Hand and machine pieced by Donna Lynn Thomas, Basehor, KS, machine quilted by Kelly Ashton, Overland Park, KS, 2007.

The curves in this lovely water-colored quilt are easy to sew and master. The pinwheel border is a simple but effective addition to the design.

Missouri Riverboat Paddles

Block size: 10" finished size
Number of blocks: 5

. . . .

Fabric Requirements:

◆ 1 yd. outer border print

◆ 3/4 yd. blue print for block and border piecing

◆ 3/4 yd. batik for block and border piecing

◆ 1 yd. light blue print

◆ 1/2 yd. green print for block circles and thin borders

◆ 1/2 yd. teal print for side set triangles

◆ 1/2 yd. for binding

◆ 3 3/8 yds. for backing

You will also need appliqué supplies to include thread to match the green print and a small amount of template plastic or freezer paper to make the circle shape. If you have preferred appliqué methods that differ from those provided in this book, please feel free to use them in lieu of mine.

. . . .

Cutting Instructions:

Note: Be sure to mark Templates A, B and C face down on the wrong side of the fabric.

From both the blue print and the batik print, cut:

◆ 20 Template A

◆ 56 Template E OR 28 - 3 3/8" squares

From the light blue print, cut:

◆ 20 Template B

◆ 20 Template C

◆ 112 Template E OR 56 - 3 3/8" squares

From the green print, cut:

◆ 5 Template D (mark on right side of fabric for appliqué)

◆ 7 - 1 1/2" x 42" strips

From the teal print, cut:

◆ 1 -16" square cut ⊠ for side set triangles

◆ 2 - 8 1/2" squares cut ◻ for corner triangles

From the outer border print, cut:

5- 5 1/2" x 42" strips

. . . .

Assembly Instructions:

Refer to special skills sections on:

◆ Curved piecing, p. 28

◆ Integrated Piecing on p. 31

◆ Quick Triangles p. 25

1. Sew a blue A to a light blue B as shown. Make 4. Sew a batik A to a light blue C as shown. Make 4.

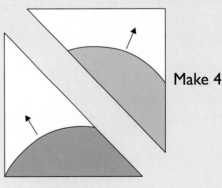

Make 4

Make 4

2. Sew the 2 pieced triangles together as shown to make a square. Make 4.

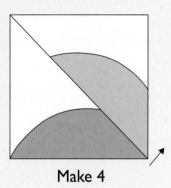

Make 4

3. Sew the squares together as shown to complete a block. Make 5 Paddle blocks.

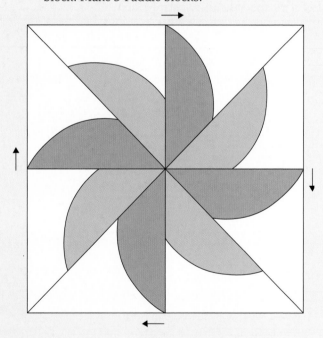

4. Turn under and baste the raw edges of the green circle. Appliqué the green circle over the center of each block. Be sure to use thread to closely match the green print.

5. Sew the Paddle blocks, teal side-set triangles, and corner triangles into rows as shown. Join the rows together to complete the quilt center.

6. Sew the seven 1 1/2" x 42" green strips together end to end following the instructions for Plain Borders on p. 35. Cut 2 strips to fit the center middle of the quilt top. Sew these to opposite sides of the quilt and press. Measure and cut 2 strips to fit the center width of the top, including the green borders. Sew these to the top and bottom of the quilt. Press. Reserve the excess border stripping for the second green border.

7. Sew a blue triangle E to a light blue triangle E to make a square. Make 4. [Note: If you rotary cut 3 3/8" squares, you need to either make quick-triangles by hand from the squares (see p.25 for more information) or cut them on the diagonal to make half-square triangles that you then sew into pairs as per the Template E pieces.] Sew the 4 pieced squares together as shown to make a Pinwheel block. Make 14 Pinwheel blocks. Press the seams on the back in a clockwise direction.

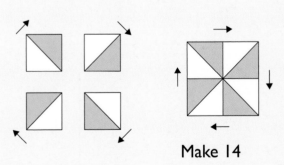

Make 14

8. Using the 56 batik triangle E and remaining 56 light blue triangle E pieces (or the 3 3/8" squares cut on the diagonal or sewn into quick triangles), repeat step 7 to make 14 batik/light blue Pinwheel blocks.

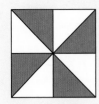

9. Alternately sew 3 batik and 3 blue Pinwheel blocks together to make 2 side borders. Measure the borders through the middle of the quilt. If they are too long, take tiny seams between blocks in multiple places along the border to reduce the length. Pin and sew in place. Be careful to orient the borders properly on the sides so that the pinwheels will alternate by color around the quilt. Refer to the photo for guidance.

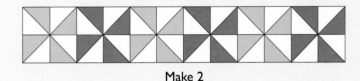

Make 2

10. Repeat step 9 for the top and bottom Pinwheel borders, using 4 batik and 4 blue Pinwheel blocks for each border.

Make 2

11. Following the directions for Plain Borders on p. 35, sew the second green and the outer borders in place.

12. Layer, baste and quilt as desired.

13. Bind with six 2 1/4"-wide cross-grain double fold binding strips.

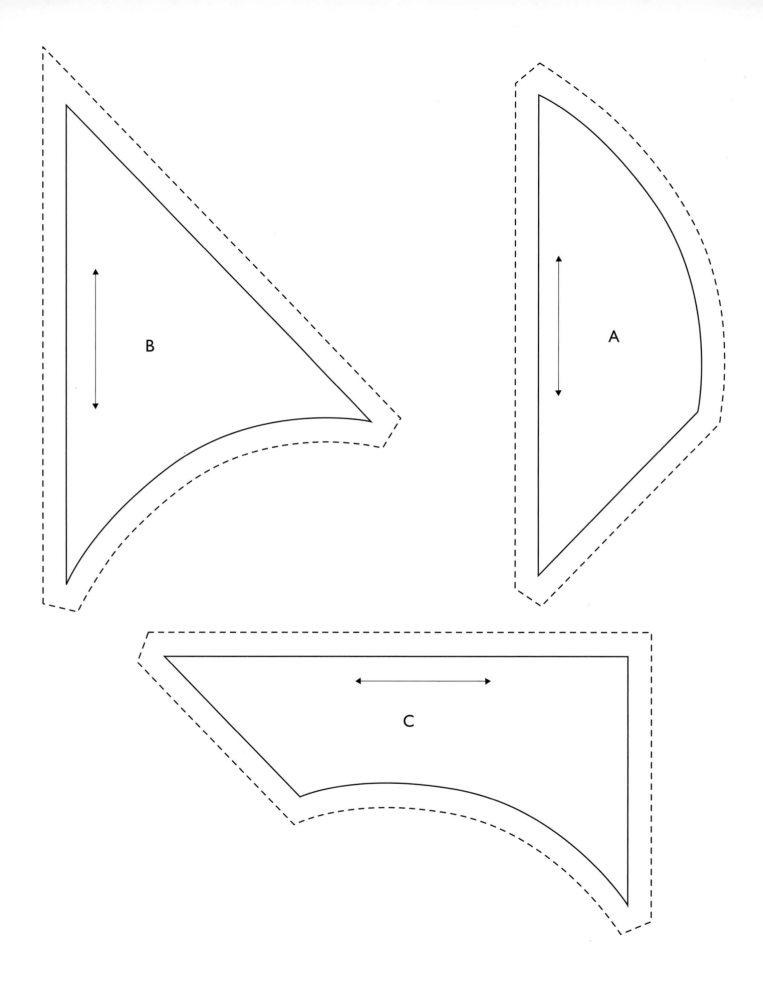

B

A

C

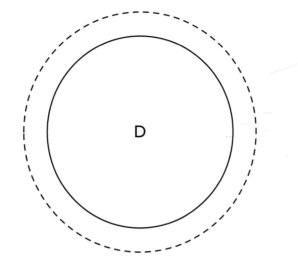

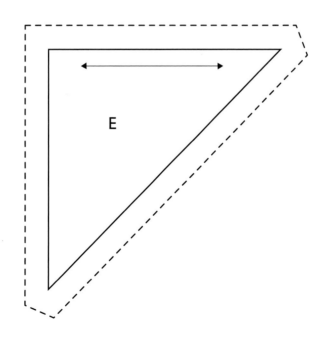

Mother's Stars in Heaven

Quilt Size: 63" square

*Hand and machine pieced by Donna Lynn Thomas, Basehor, KS, hand quilted by Aline
Duerr, Jeffersonville, KY, 2006*

The LeMoyne star blocks in this quilt were hand pieced over many years while holding
vigil for my mother during her many trips to ICU with emphysema. For 15 years I collected
border prints and directional fabrics with interesting repeats. Then using mirrors to find
different repeats, I cut 8 diamonds from the same position on the print to create fascinating
kaleidoscope designs. One half-yard of fabric can produce one or more blocks. It's a
technique I picked up in the mid-1980's while learning to make octagonal boxes with glued
fabric coverings. Over the years, I made many more than the 25 blocks featured in the quilt
shown here. My mother has passed on but her memory is always with me in this quilt.

Purple Stars

Table mat size: 24" square
Hand pieced and hand quilted by
Donna Lynn Thomas, Basehor, KS,
2005

Four of the purple blocks leftover from the quilt above were cut from the same border print. By cutting different repeats, the four blocks are completely different. These mirrored stars can be quite addictive.

Two Color Star

Mat size: 14 1/2" square
Hand pieced and hand quilted by
Donna Lynn Thomas, Basehor, KS,
2006

You don't need border prints to make the LeMoyne star as this two print version proves. I enjoy making one block mats for my tables or to sew into pillows or just for fun!

LeMoyne Star

Block Size: 8 1/2"

Number of blocks: 25

Fabric Requirements:

- ❖ 12 - 13 half yd. pieces of assorted border or repeat prints for the stars (depending on the repeat you should get at least 2 blocks from one print) OR 1 - 11" piece of a darker print for each of the 25 stars if you choose NOT to use repeating prints

- ❖ 10" x 14" piece of 25 light prints

- ❖ 1 5/8 yd. dark brown print for side-set triangles and borders

- ❖ 1 1/4 yd. multicolor light print for border

- ❖ 1/2 yd. for binding

- ❖ 4 yds. for backing

In addition, if you plan to use mirrors, you will need to purchase a set of double mirrors hinged together. They are available through most quilt shops.

Cutting Instructions:

See below for instructions on cutting diamonds using mirrors.

From each of the star prints, cut:

- ❖ 8 Template A (cut 2 sets of 8 from different repeats if you are cutting 2 stars from each print)

From each of the 25 light prints, cut:

- ❖ 4 Template B
- ❖ 4 Template C

From the dark brown print, cut:

- ❖ 8 - 1 1/4" x 9" sashing strips
- ❖ 2 - 1 1/4" x 10 1/2" sashing strips
- ❖ 2 - 1 1/4" x 29" sashing strips
- ❖ 15 - 1 1/2" x 42" strips for the 2nd, 4th, and 6th borders
- ❖ 1 - 14 3/4" square cut ⊠ for the side-set triangles
- ❖ 2 - 8 1/4" squares, cut ◩ for the corner triangles

From the multicolor light print, cut:

- ❖ 4 - 2 7/8" x 42" strips for the inner border
- ❖ 6 - 4 1/2" x 42" strips for the 5th border

1. To cut the diamonds using mirrors, place the finished size diamond template on the right sides of the fabric at a desirable repeat in the print. Without moving the template, carefully place the hinged mirrors around the two sides of the diamond as shown in the photo.

2. Now remove the diamond template and the reflection in the mirror will preview the repeat for you. If you like it, replace the template and put pins in the fabric at the two sharp points.

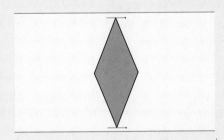

3. Turn the fabric over and replace the template on the wrong side of the repeat matching the points to the pins. Trace around the diamond and cut it out 1/4" from the marked lines. Using this first cut diamond as your guide, cut 7 more diamonds from the exact same repeat.

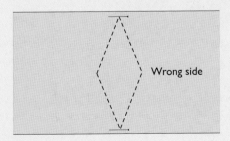

Assembly Instructions:

Refer to special skills sections on:

◈ Multiple Center Seams on p. 29

◈ Set-in Seams on p. 26

1. Sew 8 matching diamonds into 4 pairs. Be careful to align and pin matching reference points along the seams if you are using repeats. Sew the pairs into 2 groups of 4 to make half-blocks. Sew the half-blocks together to make a LeMoyne Star.

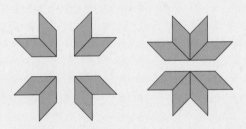

2. Set in 4 light triangles and 4 light squares to complete the block. Press all seams in a consistent circular fashion, either clockwise or counter clockwise. Repeat Steps 1 and 2 to make a total of 25 LeMoyne Star blocks.

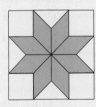

3. Lay out 5 LeMoyne Star blocks with the dark brown sashing strips and 4 side-set triangles as shown.

4. Sew the pieces into rows. Join the rows together. Sew the 4 dark brown corner triangles to the corners of the quilt center. The side-set triangles are oversized because the center of the quilt needs to measure 27 3/4" square at this point, including seam allowances. Trim it down to this size.

5. Following the general instructions on pp. 35 for Plain Borders, sew the 2 7/8" light multi-color inner border and the 1 1/2" dark brown second border in place. The quilt should now measure 34 1/2" including seam allowances.

6. Sew 4 LeMoyne Star blocks together to make a pieced side border. Make 2. Sew them to the sides of the quilt top.

7. Sew 6 LeMoyne Star blocks together to make a pieced border. Make 2. Sew them to the top and bottom of the quilt top.

8. Following the general instructions on pp. 35 for Plain Borders, sew the dark brown, multicolor light and brown outer borders to the quilt to complete the top.

9. Layer, baste and quilt as desired.

10. Bind with 7 - 2 1/4"-wide cross-grain double fold binding strips.

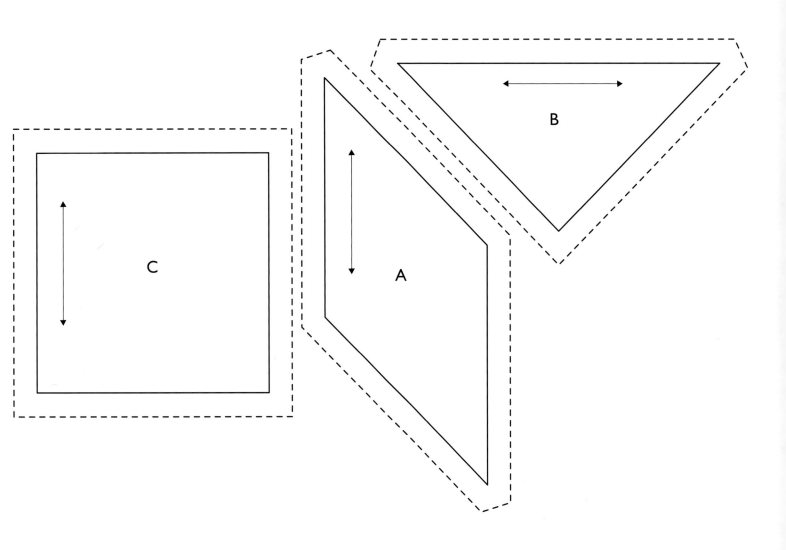

- -

Diamonds in the Window

Quilt Size: 53 1/2" square

Hand and machine pieced and machine quilted by M. Deborah Rose, Lansing KS, 2007

Primary colors with black are always a winning combination and this quilt is no exception. The Diamonds in the Window block has only four pieces but sewn together into groups of four, the block becomes quite interesting. This block has a lot of potential for all kinds of interesting setting ideas. Make some blocks and see what new sets you might come up with!

Diamonds in the Window

Block size: 4"
Number of blocks: 100

Fabric Requirements:

- ◈ 1/4 yd. or 1 fat quarter each of 2 red, 2 blue, 2 gold and 2 green prints
- ◈ 5/8 yd. each of 4 black prints
- ◈ 1/3 yd. light print
- ◈ 3/4 yd. black print for inner and outer borders
- ◈ 3/8 yd. for binding
- ◈ 3 1/4 yds. for backing

Cutting Requirements:

Since this quilt mixes rotary cut and template cut pieces, it is important to have measured 1/4" seam allowances when cutting out the template-marked pieces. See p. 31 on Integrated Piecing for more information.

From each of the red, blue, gold and green prints, cut:

- ◈ 13 Template A (you need a total of 25 from each color family)
- ◈ 8 - 2 1/2" squares for border piecing

From each of the 4 black prints, cut:

- ◈ 25 Template A-R
- ◈ 13 - 3 3/8" squares for block piecing (you need a total of 50 squares from all 4 prints)
- ◈ 7 - 4 1/4" squares cut ⊠ for the pieced border
- ◈ 4 - 2 3/8 " squares cut ⊿ for the pieced border

From the light print, cut,

- ◈ 50 - 3 3/8" squares for block piecing

From the black border print, cut:

- ◈ 10 - 2 1/2" x 42" strips for inner and outer borders

Assembly Instructions:

Refer to special skills sections on:

- ◈ Mitered Seams, p. 30
- ◈ Quick Triangles, p. 25
- ◈ Integrated Piecing, p. 31

1. Referring to p. 27 on Quick Triangles, draw a center diagonal line on the wrong side of a light 3 3/8" square. Draw a sewing line 1/4" on each side of the center line. Place a light 3 3/8" square atop a black square with right sides together, matching carefully. Pin then sew on the 1/4" lines. Cut apart and press to make 2 pieced squares as shown. Repeat for all 50 black and light 3 3/8" squares.

Make 100

2. Sew a red piece (Template A) to the light side of the pieced square as shown. If you are working by hand, remember to mark back a 1/4" sewing line on the light side of the seam for matching purposes.

3. In the same fashion as Step 2, sew a black piece (Template A-R) to the other light side of the pieced square as shown.

4. To miter the corner seam joining A to A-R, fold the block in half on the diagonal, right sides together as shown. Match the corner sewing lines, pin and stitch from point to point to complete a Diamond in the Window block.

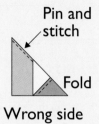

Pin and stitch

Fold

Wrong side

5. Repeating Steps 2 - 4 make 25 red, blue, green and gold Diamond in the Window blocks for a total of 100 blocks.

Make 100

6. Referring closely to the diagram, carefully lay out your blocks into 10 rows of 10 blocks so the colors flow across the diagonal of the quilt. It is helpful to pin all the blocks to a design wall. If you do not have one, lay out one row at a time and label the rows so you do not get the order confused. Sew the rows together, pressing alternately from row to row. Join the rows together to complete the center of the quilt.

7. Following the general instructions on p. 35 for Plain Borders, sew the inner black border in place.

8. Set aside 4 green, 4 gold and 4 red 2 1/2" squares. Center and sew 2 black half-square triangles and 1 black quarter-square triangle to each of the green and gold set-aside squares as shown to make 8 border end units. Remember to center the triangles on the squares by finger pressing fold marks in the center of both the triangle and the square. Match the fold marks and pin to align the pieces before sewing.

Make 4 gold   Make 4 green

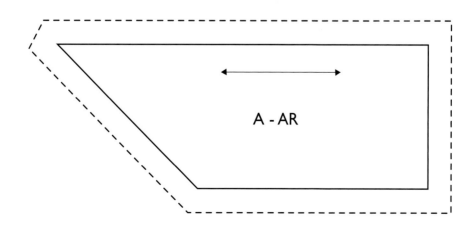

Make 4 pieced borders

9. Center and sew black half-square triangles to the 4 sides of each set-aside red square to make 4 border corner squares.

10. Sew a black quarter-square triangle to opposite sides of one of the remaining 2 1/2" squares as shown to make a border side-unit. Repeat for all of the remaining 2 1/2 " squares.

11. Lay out 4 blue side units, 3 gold side units, 3 red side units and 3 green side units as shown. Sew them together to make a border strip. Sew a green and gold end unit to each end to complete a border. Repeat to make 4 pieced borders.

12. Measure the 4 borders against the center measurement of the quilt top. If they are too big, take in small amounts on many seams to adjust the length. Once adjusted, sew 2 of the borders to the sides of the quilt top.

13. Sew a red border corner square to each end of the 2 remaining borders. Sew the last two pieced borders to the top and bottom of the quilt. Adjust border length in as necessary as in step 12.

14. Following the general instructions on pp. 35 for Plain Borders, sew the black outer border in place to complete the quilt top.

15. Layer, baste and quilt as desired.

16. Bind with 2 1/4"-wide cross-grain double fold binding strips.

A - AR

Stars Dipped in Chocolate

Stars Dipped in Chocolate

Quilt Size: 79" square

Hand and machine pieced by Donna Lynn Thomas, Basehor, KS, machine quilted by Kelly Ashton, Overland Park, KS 2007

This rich looking quilt is all based around the wonderful border print fabric used in the sashings and borders. Many, many yards (about 9) were required in order to fussy cut the sashing strips and borders just the way I wanted. Also, I had planned three borders for the quilt, but the repeat border print provided me with two of them in one cut. As a result, that border is mitered which I normally do not do unless required as in this situation. The pattern is written for a more conventional use of prints, as it is unlikely you will find a printed border fabric with the same dimensions and features as the one I used.

Rising Star

Block Size: 12"
Number of blocks: 13

Fabric Requirements:

- ◆ 1 7/8 yds. brown print for block piecing and outer border
- ◆ 5/8 yd. red print #1 for block piecing
- ◆ 7/8 yd. plum print for block piecing and sashing squares
- ◆ 2 3/8 yd. cream print for block piecing and side-set triangles
- ◆ 1 yd. yellow print for block piecing
- ◆ 2 1/8 yds. red print #2 for sashings and middle border
- ◆ 3/4 yd. brown and tan print for inner border
- ◆ 5 yds. backing print
- ◆ 3/4 yd. binding print

Cutting Instructions:

This pattern is a chance for you to try hand-piecing rotary cut blocks and folded corner units. All cutting instructions are for rotary cutting and no templates are provided.

From the brown print, cut:

- ◆ 9 - 3 1/2" x 42" strips, crosscut into 104 squares for folded corners
- ◆ 8 - 3 1/2" x 42" strips for the outer border

From red print #1, cut:

- ◆ 2 - 3 1/2" x 42" strips crosscut into 13 squares for block piecing
- ◆ 5 - 2" x 42" strips crosscut into 104 squares for folded corners

From the plum print, cut:

- ◆ 7 - 3 1/2" x 42" strips, crosscut into 76 squares for block piecing and sashing squares

From the cream print, cut:

- ◆ 5 - 2" x 42" strips, crosscut into 52 - 2" x 3 1/2" rectangles for folded corners
- ◆ 3 - 2" x 42" strips, crosscut into 52 squares for block piecing
- ◆ 2 - 23" squares cut ⊠ to make 8 side-set triangles
- ◆ 2 - 14 1/2" squares, cut ◻ to make 4 corner triangles

From the yellow print, cut:

- ◆ 9 - 3 1/2" x 42" strips, crosscut into 52 - 3 1/2" x 6 1/2" rectangles for folded corners

From red print #2, cut:

- ◆ 12 - 3 1/2" x 42" strips, crosscut into 36 - 3 1/2" x 12 1/2" sashing strips (if you are fussy cutting a repeat, you will not cut 12 strips but rather long lengths of strips parallel to the selvage containing your desired repeat; then cut the repeats individually)
- ◆ 8 - 3 1/2" x 42" strips for the middle border

From the brown and tan print, cut:

- ◆ 8 - 3 1/2" x 42" strips for the outer border

Assembly Instructions:

Refer to special skills sections on:

- ◆ Folded Corners on p. 25
- ◆ Integrated Piecing on p. 31

1. Referring to Folded Corners on p. 25, mark diagonal sewing lines on the wrong side of 2 small red squares. Place one red square on the corner of a cream print rectangle oriented as shown. Sew on the diagonal line by either hand or machine. Press to the red and trim away the excess corner underneath 1/4" from the sewing line. Repeat for the adjacent corner as shown. Make 4.

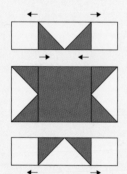

Make 4

2. Lay out 1 red 3 1/2" square, 2" cream squares, and the 4 units from Step 1 as shown. Sew the units into rows and join the rows together to make the block center. If you are sewing by hand, mark back 1/4" sewing lines on one side of each seam before you pin and sew it.

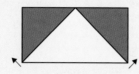
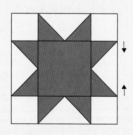

3. Referring to Folded Corners on p. 25 and Step 1 above, make 4 brown and yellow folded corner units as shown.

Make 4

4. Lay out the red star from Step 2, 4 plum squares, and the 4 brown and yellow folded corner units from Step 3 as shown. Sew the units into rows and join the rows together to make 1 Star Within a Star block. Repeat Steps 1-4 to make 12 more blocks.

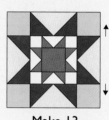
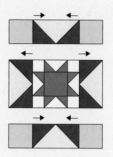

Make 13

5. Lay out the 13 completed blocks and the 36 red sashing strips and 24 plum sashing squares as shown. Join them into block rows and sashing rows.

6. Join the sashing rows to the block rows as shown. Lay the side-set triangles at the ends of the rows, orienting them carefully as in the diagram.

7. Join the rows together. Sew the 4 cream corner triangles to the corners of the quilt. Trim the quilt top to 1/4" from the sashing square points.

8. Following the general instructions on pp. 35 for Plain Borders, sew the inner brown and tan, the red and the outer brown borders to the quilt top.

9. Layer, baste and quilt as desired.

10. Bind with 9 - 2 1/4"-wide cross-grain double fold binding strips.

Winding Paths

Quilt size: 50" square

Hand and machine pieced by Donna Lynn Thomas, Basehor, KS, machine quilted by Kelly Ashton, Overland Park, KS, 2007

These simple Split Nine-Patch blocks can be rotated in a myriad of ways to create many intricate looking designs. Equally inviting with a fixed palette or scraps, the simple construction of this block makes it fun to sew. Pattern provided.

Autumn Walk in the Woods

Quilt size: 72" square

Machine pieced by Donna Lynn Thomas, Doylestown, PA, machine quilted by Charlotte Freeman, Ridgecrest, CA, 1999

Adding another round of 'paths' makes a larger version of the quilt. This fat quarter friendly scrap quilt was made ten blocks at a time using a different set of prints with each of ten different groups. Each group of ten is made from one collection of 5-6 prints (the black and light for the triangles, the two main prints and the two accent prints). Once done, those ten blocks will be exact duplicates of each other. When you make the next set of ten, choose a new set of prints in the same colors and use them in the same positions. Each set of ten blocks has the same color usage but a completely different set of prints.

Winding Paths table topper

Quilt size: 35 1/2" square

Hand and machine pieced by Donna Lynn Thomas, Basehor, KS, machine quilted by Sandy Gore, Liberty, MO, 2007

Quick and easy to make, this scrappy little table topper goes together in a snap. Sixteen blocks are made in groups of four with four different sets of prints.

Peaceful Paths

Quilt size: 47" square

Machine pieced and hand quilted by M. Deborah Rose, Lansing, KS, 2007

Elegant Japanese prints give this stunning quilt a completely different look.

Winding Paths

Block size: 6" finished size
Number of blocks: 36

Fabric Requirements:

- 1 1/4 yd. medium blue print for wide border and block piecing
- 1 yd. navy print for narrow borders and block piecing
- 5/8 yd. sage green for block piecing
- 3/4 yd. pink print for narrow border and block piecing
- 3/8 yd blue/green batik for block piecing
- 1/2 yd. white print for block piecing
- 1/2 yd. for binding
- 3 3/8 yds. for backing

Cutting Instructions:

From the medium blue print, cut:

- 36 Template A OR 36 - 2 1/2" squares
- *144 Template C OR 144 - 1 1/2" squares
- 5 - 4 1/2" x 42" strips for the wide border

From the navy print, cut:

- 108 Template B OR 54 - 2 7/8" squares
- 9 - 1 1/2" x 42" strips for inner and outer borders

From the sage green print, cut:

- 36 Template A OR 36 - 2 1/2" squares
- *144 Template C OR 144 - 1 1/2" squares

From the pink print, cut:

- *144 Template C OR 144 - 1 1/2" squares

- 5 - 1 1/2" x 42" strips for third border

From the blue/green batik, cut:

- *144 Template C OR 144 - 1 1/2" squares

From the white print, cut:

- 108 Template B OR 54 - 2 7/8" squares

*Note: If you prefer to strip piece the four-patch units, please substitute the 144 cut squares with 6 - 1 1/2" x 42" strips from each of the 4 prints asterisked. Skip Steps 1 and 2 below and assemble the 2 types of strip units as shown in the diagram. Make 6 strip units of each color combination and cut a total of 144 - 1 1/2" wide segments from each color combination. Sew them into like-colored pairs to make 72 four-patch units as shown.

Assembly Instructions

to make 1 Split Nine-Patch block:

- Refer to special skills sections on:
- Quick Triangles on p. 25

1. Sew 2 small medium blue squares and 2 small pink squares together to make a four-patch unit as shown. Make 2 four-patch units.

Make 2

2. Repeat step 1 using 2 small batik squares and 2 small sage squares. Make 2 four-patch units.

Make 2

3. Cut the navy and white 2 7/8" squares in half on the diagonal to make 108 half-square triangles. Sew a navy triangle to a white triangle. Make 3 pieced squares. Note: You may opt to use the uncut 2 7/8" squares to make quick triangles by hand. Refer to p. 33 for more information.

Make 3

4. Lay out the 3 pieced squares, the 2 blue/pink four-patch units, 2 batik/sage four-patch units, 1 medium blue A, and 1 sage green A as shown. Sew into rows and then join the rows together.

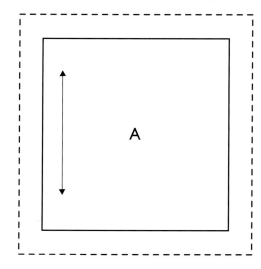

Make 36

5. Repeat Steps 1-4 to make 36 blocks.

6. After orienting the blocks as shown in the diagram, sew the blocks into rows. Press the seams in alternate directions from row to row. Join the rows together to form the quilt center. Tip: Forget about the rest of the block and just focus on the dark/light contrast of the triangles and their diagonal direction as your orientation guide.

7. Following the general instructions on pp. 35 for Plain Borders, sew the navy blue, medium blue, pink and navy blue borders to the quilt top.

8. Layer, baste and quilt as desired.

9. Bind with five 2 1/4"-wide cross-grain double fold binding strips.

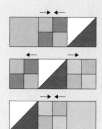

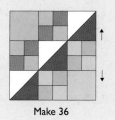

Simple Stars

Quilt Size: 33 1/2" x 42"

Hand pieced by Donna Lynn Thomas, Basehor, KS, machine quilted by Kim Pope, Pipersville, PA 2007

Red, black and tan reproduction prints were the inspiration for this inviting quilt. Each of the 12 red stars and 6 black stars is sewn with a different pair of prints and set on point without sashings. The Simple Star block is similar to the Periwinkle block on p. 100 except for the use of set-in seams as opposed to curved seams and the location of the block points. Simple to piece, as indicated by its name, this block can be colored in many ways to create totally different looks.

Tropical Stars

Quilt size: 46" square

Hand pieced by Donna Lynn Thomas, Basehor, KS, machine quilted by Sandy Gore, Liberty, MO, 2007

By using four different prints for the sides of the block and sewing the blocks into groups of four then setting the groups on point, the quilt takes on a completely different 3-dimensional look—you'd never know it was the same block. Bright contemporary colors and prints were just right for this design. Pattern notes provided.

Oh My Stars!

Quilt size: 34" square

Hand pieced and machine quilted by Katherine Brigham, West Chester, PA 2007

Kathy began piecing her blocks by machine but quickly scrapped them and moved to hand piecing because of its accuracy. She so enjoyed the hand piecing process that she went on to sew the side-setting triangles by hand also. The beautiful batiks in this quilt showcase the design just perfectly and the pieced binding brings the colors back out to the edge without the use of borders.

Dare to be Different

Quilt size: 47 1/2" square

Hand and machine pieced and machine quilted by Doris Brown, Lansing, KS 2007

    Set straight, all the red stars fade to become the background with Doris' careful placement of color on the sides of the blocks. The newly formed brown, blue, green, tan and yellow pinwheels, come to the forefront instead of the stars as in the other quilt samples. What another innovative way to use such a very basic block.

Simple Stars

Block size: 6"

Number of blocks: 18

Fabric Requirements:

❖ 9" square each of 12 red prints and 6 black prints

❖ 8" x 11" piece each of 18 light or tan prints

❖ 1/2 yd. black print for side-set triangles

❖ 1/4 yd. red print for the inner border

❖ 1/6 yd. black solid for middle border

❖ 1/2 yd. tan, red and black print for outer border

❖ 3/8 yd. binding

❖ 1 1/8 yd. backing

Variation Note: To make the Tropical Stars version, you need 5/8 yd. for the stars, a fat quarter each of 3 accent prints, 11/2 yds. of black solid for block piecing, side-set triangles and the outer border, and 1/4 yd. extra of one of the accent prints for the middle border.

Cutting Instructions:

From each of the red and black prints, cut:

❖ 4 Template B

From each of the light/tan prints, cut:

❖ 4 Template A

From the black print, cut:

❖ 3 -10" squares cut ⊠ for side-set triangles

❖ 2 - 5 1/2" squares cut ◿ for corner triangles

From the red print, cut:

❖ 4 - 1 1/2" x 42" strips for the inner border

From the black solid, cut:

❖ 4 - 1" x 42" strips for the middle border

From the tan, red and black print, cut:

❖ 4 - 3" x 42" strips for the outer border

Variation Note: For the Tropical Stars quilt, you need 80 Template B from your star fabric, 20 Template A from each of the accent prints and the black solid, 1 - 18 1/2" black square for the side-setting triangles, 2 - 9 1/2" black squares for the corner triangles, 4 - 2"-wide strips for the inner border, and 5 - 5"-wide black strips for the outer border.

Assembly Instructions:

Refer to special skills section on:

❖ Set-in Seams on p. 26

1. Sew 4 matching Template B pieces together as shown to make a star. Make 12 red and 6 black stars.

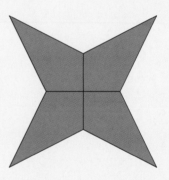

2. Referring to p. 26 on Set-in Seams, sew a Template A triangle to one side of a star. Repeat with a continuous thread to attach the rest of the triangles in succession around the star. Repeat on all stars to complete the blocks.

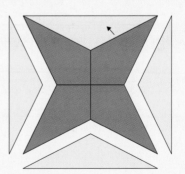

Variation note: Even if you are using different accent prints on the sides, the process is the same. Refer to the photograph and carefully add the accents in the correct order. You will need to make 20 blocks.

3. Lay out the blocks in a pleasing on-point set. Lay the black side-set and corner triangles in place at the ends of the rows and sew the blocks and side-set triangles into rows as shown.

Variation note: Sew the 20 blocks into five groups of 4. Be careful to orient the blocks properly before sewing them into 4-block units. Refer to the photos and lay out the 4-block units with the side-set triangles and sew into rows. Trim the quilt edges as in Step 4 and add the pink and black borders.

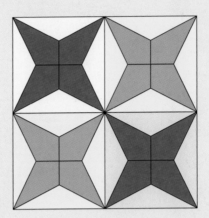

4. Trim the edges of the quilt top to 1/4" from the block points and square off the corners.

5. Following the general instructions on pp. 35 for Plain Borders, sew the red, black and light borders in place.

6. Layer, baste and quilt as desired.

7. Bind with 4 - 2 1/4" cross-grain double fold binding strips.

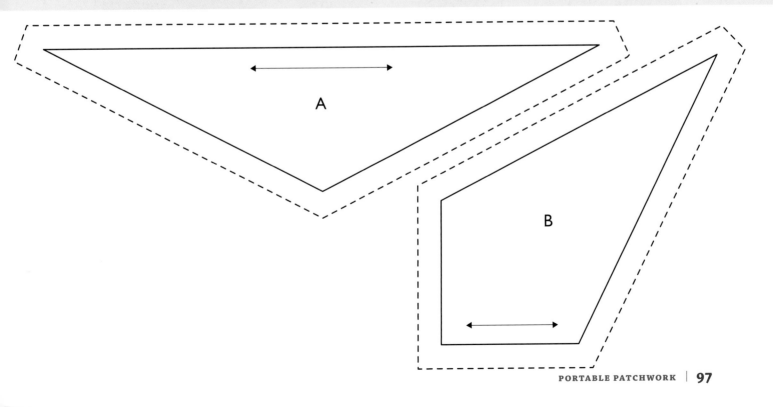

Periwinkle Patch

Periwinkle Patch

Quilt size: 25 1/2" square

Hand pieced and hand quilted by Donna Lynn Thomas, Basehor, KS 2007

The simple curves of this traditional Periwinkle block make for quick piecing of this pretty table topper. Made entirely from charm pack squares and scraps plus a little yardage for the borders, you could easily just keep on cutting and piecing blocks to make a large quilt. The blocks work up quickly and with bits of time here and there, you'd suddenly find yourself one day with a nice stack of blocks for a big quilt. Pattern provided.

Sweet Treat

Quilt size: 13" square

Hand pieced and hand quilted by Donna Lynn Thomas, Basehor, KS, 2006

A variation on the simple Periwinkle block divides the center unit into quarters allowing for a little more intricacy to the block. Again, a collection of charm squares was the inspiration for this table mat. A small amount of yardage (fat quarters work well) was needed for the light pieces and borders.

Periwinkle Patch

Block size: 5"
Number of blocks: 16

Fabric Requirements

- ◈ 17 dark 5" charm squares
- ◈ 32 light 5" charm squares or 16 - 6 1/2" light squares
- ◈ 1/8 yd. brown print for inner border
- ◈ 3/8 yd. stripe for outer border
- ◈ 1/4 yd for binding
- ◈ 7/8 yd. for backing

Note: If you wish to make the quartered Periwinkle instead of the one-piece block, you still need the same number of charm squares

Cutting Instructions:

From each of the 16 dark charm squares, cut:

- ◈ 1 Template A (or, for the quartered block, cut 4 Template C from each charm square)

From the 17th dark charm square, cut:

- ◈ 4 - 2 1/2" squares for the outer border corner squares

From the light charm squares, cut:

- ◈ 64 Template B (you can cut 2 B from each 5" charm square, and 4 B from a 6 1/2" square)

From the brown print, cut:

- ◈ 3 - 1 1/4" x 42" strips for the inner borders

From the stripe print, cut:

- ◈ 4 - 2 1/2" x 42" strips for the outer border

Assembly Instructions:

Refer to special skills section on:

- ◈ Curved Seams on p. 28

1. Skip this step if you are making the one-piece Periwinkle block. Sew 4 assorted Template C units together as shown to make a quartered A. Make 16.

2. Referring to p. 28 on Curved Seams, clip, center and pin a Template B to one side of a Template A or quartered A from step 1. Sew the seam and backstitch at the end in the point. Without breaking the thread, pin the next B in place. Stitch to the other side, backstitch and again don't break the thread. Repeat the process to sew all 4 B corner units in place with a continuous seam to complete a block. Make 16 blocks.

3. Sew the blocks together in a pleasing 4 x 4 set. Be careful to pin the points before sewing in order to make sharp points.

4. Following the general instructions on pp. 35 for Plain Borders, sew the brown borders to the quilt top.

5. Measure and cut the 4 outer border strips to fit the center length of the quilt top. Sew two of them to opposite sides of the quilt. Sew a 2 1/2" square to each end of the 2 remaining border strips. Sew these to the top and bottom to complete the quilt.

6. Layer, baste, and quilt as desired.

7. Bind with 3 - 2 1/4" cross-grain double fold binding strips.

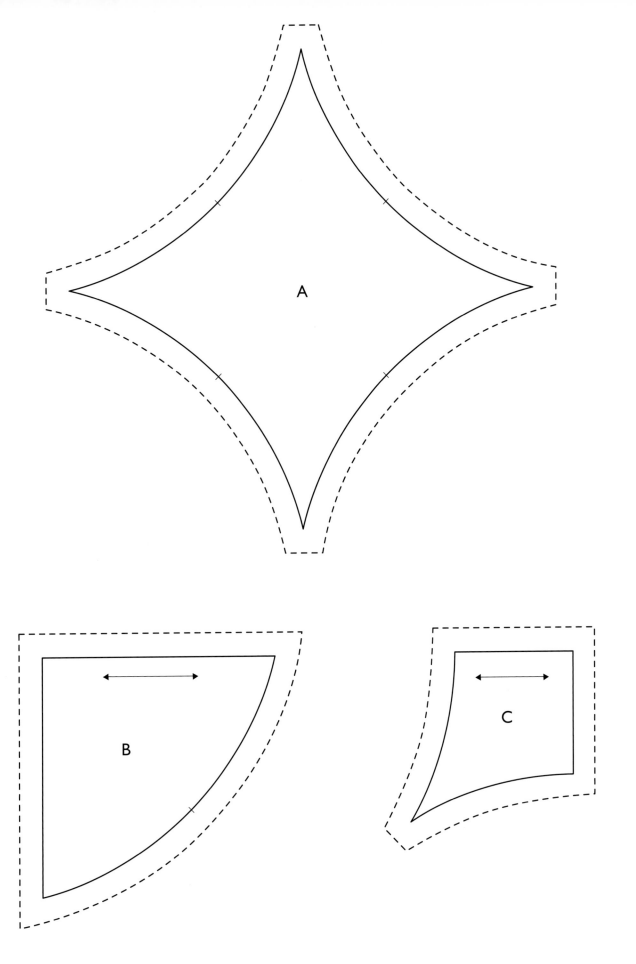

A

B

C

Mariner's Compass 🧵🧵

Mariner's Compass

Quilt Size: 71 1/4" square

Hand and machine pieced by Donna Lynn Thomas, Basehor, KS, machine quilted by Don Sutcliffe, Peculiar, MO, 2007

Pieced by hand, the complex looking Mariner's Compass blocks never gave me any trouble. I chose to appliqué the compasses to large background squares in this quilt. Since I do not like paper piecing, hand piecing is my method of choice for this block. For accurate machine piecing, I recommend marking sewing lines with finished size templates, pinning as for hand piecing, and then sewing by machine. Pattern provided.

All Things Purple Cedar Chest runner

Runner size: 28" x 56"

Hand and machine pieced by Donna Lynn Thomas, Basehor, KS, hand quilted by Aline Duerr, Jeffersonville, KY 2006

Now that my sons are grown, my extra bedrooms are going "girly". This cedar chest runner is destined for the cedar chest in my periwinkle and white guest room. I love purple and I love making Mariner's Compass blocks so it was a fun project to sew.

Mariner's Compass
Block Size: 14 1/2"
Number of blocks: 5

Fabric Requirements:

- ◈ 12" square each of 4 brick prints for compass points
- ◈ 12" square each of 4 green prints for compass points
- ◈ 1 fat quarter each of 8 blue prints for compass points
- ◈ 1 3/8 yds. light green batik for block piecing and backgrounds
- ◈ 1 1/4 yds. blue floral for outer border, sashing squares and compass centers
- ◈ 1 5/8 yds. peach print for side-set triangles and pieced border
- ◈ 1/3 yd. blue print for inner border
- ◈ 1 1/4 yds. cinnamon print for pieced border
- ◈ 5/8 yd. for binding
- ◈ 4 1/2 yds. for backing

Note: You will also need appliqué supplies to include needles and thread to match the blue floral print and the light green batik.

Cutting Instructions:

From each of the 4 brick prints, cut:
- ◈ 5 Template A

From each of the 4 green prints, cut:
- ◈ 5 Template D

From each of the 4 blue prints, cut:
- ◈ 5 Template C
- ◈ 2 - 1 3/4" x 15" strips for sashings

From the light green batik, cut:
- ◈ 80 Template B
- ◈ 5 - 15 1/2" squares for block backgrounds

Note: Cut the big squares first and then cut the template pieces from the leftover area.

From the blue floral, cut:
- ◈ 5 Template E for the compass centers
- ◈ 12 - 1 3/4" squares for sashing corners
- ◈ 7 - 5" x 42" strips for outer border

From the peach print, cut:
- ◈ 4 - 3 3/4" x 53" strips along the lengthwise selvedge for the border
- ◈ 1 - 23 3/4" square cut ⊠ for side-set triangles
- ◈ 2 - 12 1/2" squares cut ◻ for corner triangles
- ◈ 4 - 3 3/4" squares for the border corner squares

From the blue print, cut:
- ◈ 5 - 1 3/4" x 42" strips for the inner border

From the cinnamon print, cut:
- ◈ 16 - 2 1/4" x 42" strips for pieced border panels

Assembly Instructions:

1. Sew a light green B to either side of a blue C. Make 8.

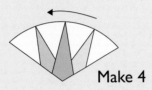

Make 8

2. Sew a B/C unit to either side of a green D. Make 4.

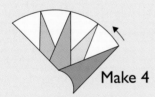

Make 4

3. Sew a B/C/D unit to the side of a brick A. Make 4 quarter-compass units.

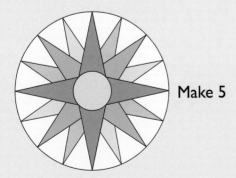

Make 4

4. Sew the 4 quarter-compass units together to make a full circle.

Make 5

5. Lightly press vertical and horizontal lines through the center of the light green background squares. Using these as orienting lines, center and appliqué the compass onto the background,

making certain the 4 brick spokes line up with the press marks. If desired, cut away the background fabric from behind the compass 1/4" from the stitching on the back. Appliqué the blue floral circle E onto the center of the compass. Using a large square ruler, trim the blocks to 15". Repeat Steps 1-5 to make a total of 5 Mariner Compass blocks.

6. Lay out the 5 blocks into rows with the assorted blue sashing strips, the blue floral sashing squares and the peach side set triangles. Sew into rows as in the diagram.

7. Sew the peach corner triangles in place to finish the quilt center.

8. Following the general instructions on pp. 35 for Plain Borders, sew the blue inner border strips to the quilt top.

9. Sew the 2 1/4"-wide cinnamon strips into 2 long border strips of 8 strips each. From the big strips, cut 4 border strips, each 53" long, letting the seams fall randomly from strip to strip. (The narrow strips and darker print will hide the seams better than the lighter peach print. That is why the light peach print is not pieced while this one is.) Reserve the leftover cinnamon stripping for later use.

10. Sew a cinnamon strip to either side of a 53" peach strip to make 4 border panels.

11. Measure and cut the 4 border panels to fit the center dimension of the quilt.

12. Sew 2 panels to the sides of the quilt top.

13. From the leftover cinnamon strips, cut 8 - 2 1/4" x 3 3/4" strips, and 8 - 2 1/4" x 7 1/4" strips. Sew a short strip to either side of a light 3 3/4" square. Sew a 7 1/4" long cinnamon strip to the top and bottom of the light square unit. Make 4 corner squares for the paneled border.

Make 4

14. Sew a corner square to the ends of the 2 remaining border panels. Sew these borders to the top and bottom of the quilt.

15. Following the general instructions on pp. 35 for Plain Borders, sew the blue floral border strips to the quilt.

16. Layer, baste and quilt as desired.

17. Bind with 8 - 2 1/4"-wide cross-grain double fold binding strips.

Variation Note for All Things Purple: Instead of one large 16" background piece, the compass backgrounds were made by sewing 4 8" squares of 4 different prints together to make each pieced 16" background. The blocks were trimmed to 15 1/2" when done. The 2" finished size pieced border was made using 40 - 2 7/8" green and 40 - 2 7/8" purple squares with the quick triangle method on p. 25. In order for the pieced border to fit, the top and side inner borders had to be cut different widths. The long borders were cut 3" wide and the short borders were cut 2" wide. The outer border was cut 2 1/2" wide.

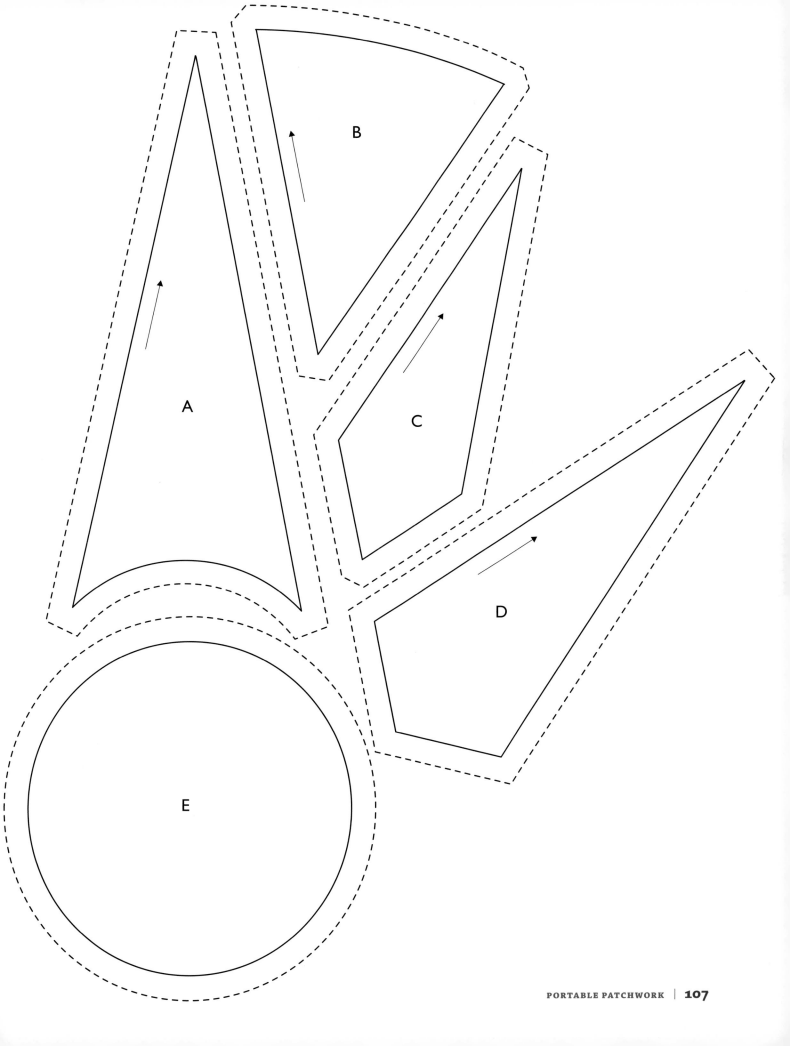

A

B

C

D

E

Spring Fling Baskets 🧵

Quilt size: 20" x 52"

Hand and machine pieced by Donna Lynn Thomas, Basehor, KS, machine quilted by Kelly Ashton, Overland Park, KS, 2007

This light-hearted quilt banner is a perfect project for those of you who would like to bring the bright colors of spring inside your home. The blocks are quite pleasant to hand piece outside in the garden enjoying the wonders of springtime or by a cozy fire in the dead of winter while you anticipate the season to come. The sawtooth border takes little time to make using the quick-triangle method either by hand or machine. Each block is made from different prints with a common unifying background print—great for using up leftovers or fabrics found in your stash.

Spring Fling Baskets

Block size: 8" square

Number of blocks: 5

Fabric Requirements:

If you have trouble getting started, begin with either the background or border print. Choose something that has lots of colors in it from which to choose prints for the baskets and flowers.

- ◈ 1/2 yd. red print for the outer border
- ◈ 1/4 yd. teal print for border
- ◈ 1 yd. light print for borders and block piecing
- ◈ 5 assorted 9" x 16" pieces for baskets
- ◈ 5 assorted 7" x 14" pieces for flower tops
- ◈ 5 assorted 7" x 14" pieces for flower bases
- ◈ 3/8 yd. for binding
- ◈ 1 5/8 yd. for backing

Cutting Instructions:

From the red print, cut:

- ◈ 4 - 3" x 42" strips for the outer border

From the teal print, cut:

- ◈ 4 - 1 1/2" x 42" strips for the third border

From the light print, cut:

- ◈ 3 - 2 1/2" x 42" strips for the inner border
- ◈ 28 - 2 7/8" squares for sawtooth border
- ◈ 5 Template A OR 3 - 4 7/8" squares cut ◹ for block piecing
- ◈ 20 Template B OR 10 - 2 7/8" squares cut ◹ for block piecing
- ◈ 10 Template C OR 10 - 2 1/2" x 4 1/2" rectangles for block piecing
- ◈ 9 Template D OR 5 - 2 1/2" squares; 5 for block piecing, 4 for sawtooth border corners

From each of the 5 assorted basket prints, cut:

- ◈ 1 Template A OR 1 4 7/8" square cut ◹ for block piecing (discard 1 triangle)
- ◈ 2 Template B OR 1 - 2 7/8" square cut ◹ for block piecing
- ◈ 1 - 2 7/8" square for the sawtooth border

From each of the 5 assorted flower top prints, cut:

- ◈ 1 Template D OR 1 - 2 1/2" square for block piecing
- ◈ 2 Template B OR 1 - 2 7/8" square cut ◹ for block piecing
- ◈ 1 - 2 7/8" square for the sawtooth border

From each of the 5 assorted flower base prints, cut:

- ◈ 1 Template E for block piecing
- ◈ 1 Template E-R for block piecing
- ◈ 1 - 2 7/8 " square for the sawtooth border

Assembly Instructions:

Refer to special skills sections on:

- ◈ Quick Triangles, p. 25.
- ◈ Template Construction on p. 8.
- ◈ Integrated Piecing on p. 35.

1. Sew a flower top B to a light B. Make 2 pieced squares as shown.

Make 2

2. Using a light square, a flower top square and the 2 pieced squares, sew the flower top together as shown.

3. Sew a light triangle B to the long edge of a flower base E and an E-R as shown. These two units will be mirror images.

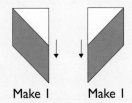

Make 1   Make 1

4. Sew the flower base to the flower top as shown. Sew a large basket triangle to the bottom of the flower.

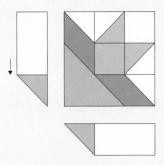

5. Sew a small basket triangle to the end of each light rectangle. Be sure to orient them carefully as in the diagram. Sew these to the bottom of the basket.

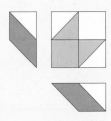

6. Sew a large light triangle to the corner of the block to complete the Basket block.

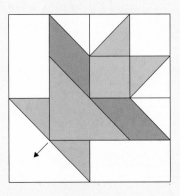

7. Repeat Steps 1-6 to make 4 more Basket blocks.

8. Following the general directions on p. xx for Plain Borders, sew the light 2 1/2" borders to the quilt.

9. Draw a diagonal line on the back of each 2 7/8" light square. Draw a sewing line 1/4" from each side of the diagonal line. Pair each light square with one of the assorted 2 7/8" print squares. Stitch on the sewing lines and cut the squares apart to make 56 pieced squares.

10. Lay out 22 pieced squares for each long side and 6 for each short side of the quilt top. Notice how the squares form a peak in the center of each border and flow from the center to the corners. Balance the colors in a pleasing manner before stitching the units into border strips. Sew a light 2 1/2" square to each end of the short borders. Measure the long pieced borders through the center of the quilt. If they are too long, take in a tiny bit on many seams throughout the border to make them fit. On the other hand if they are too short, let out tiny bits on several seams. Sew them to the sides of the quilt. Adjust the length of the short borders in the same way before sewing them to the top and bottom of the quilt top.

11. Following the general directions on p. 35 for Plain Borders, sew the teal borders to the quilt, followed by the red borders.

12. Layer, baste and quilt as desired.

13. Bind with 4 - 2 1/4"-wide cross-grain double fold binding strips.

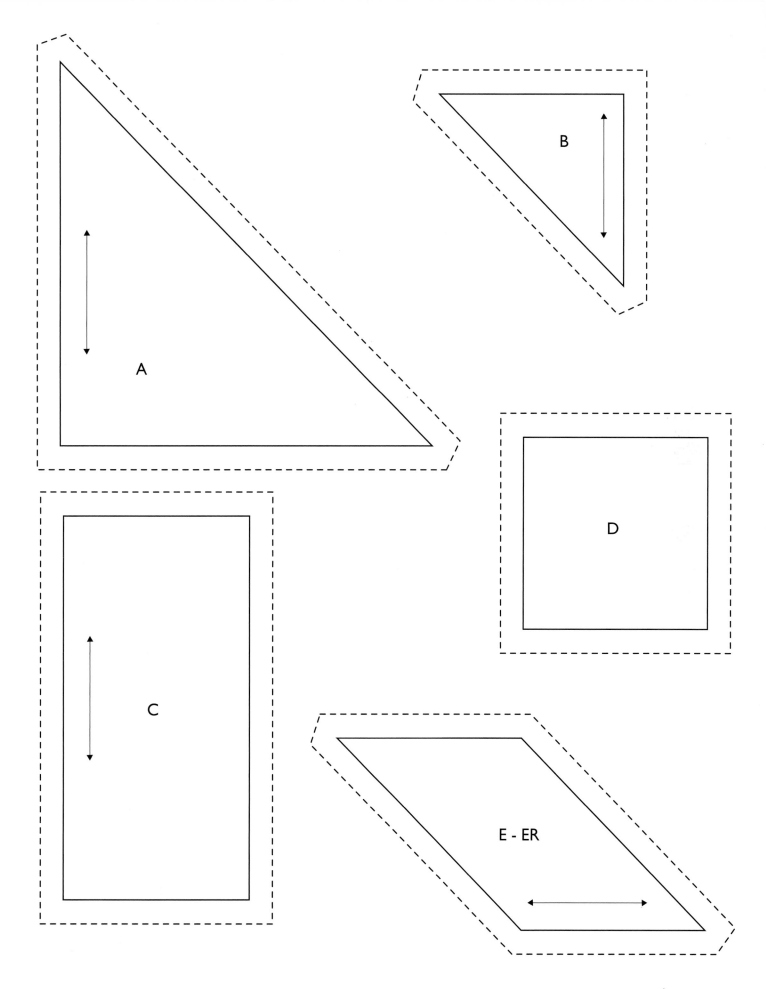

A

B

C

D

E - ER

Tree Lined Streets of Home Table Runner

19" x 53"

Hand and machine pieced by Donna Lynn Thomas, Basehor, KS, 2006. Machine quilted by Barb Fife, Overland Park, KS, 2007

Accent your table with this homey table runner. Whether in seasonal or holiday colors, the sight of houses on a tree-lined street will remind your family of the warmth and comfort of home. Pattern provided.

Tree Lined Streets of Home placemat

14" x 19"

Hand and machine pieced and hand and machine quilted by Donna Lynn Thomas, Basehor, KS 2007.

What a wonderful housewarming gift for that favorite couple or friend. As long as you're sewing, make some for your own home, as well. Simple to construct, the themes for these charming placemats are endless. Use a flat or insulated batting if they are expected to protect the table from heat. Pattern for four placemats included.

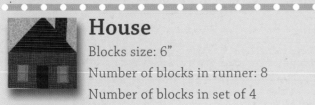

House

Blocks size: 6"

Number of blocks in runner: 8

Number of blocks in set of 4
placemats: 4

Tree

Block size: 4" x 6"

Number of blocks in runner: 12

Number of blocks in set of
4 placemats: 8

Fabric Requirements:

Table Runner:

◈ 1/4 yd. or 1 fat quarter red stripe for the roofs

◈ 1/2 yd. blue check for the houses and outer
border

◈ 1/8 yd. gold for the windows

◈ 4" x 12" piece of red print for the door

◈ 4" x 14" piece of brown print #1 for the chimney

◈ 1 fat quarter each of 4 greens for the trees

◈ 2" x 10" piece brown print #2 for the tree trunk

◈ 1/8 yd. or 1 1/8 yds of a directional print for the
"road". If the stripe runs parallel to the selvage
you will need the larger amount. Tip: If it's a print
you would be happy to have as your backing, buy
the 1 5/8 yds needed for the backing, cut the road
piece off the selvage edge and use the remaining
yardage for your backing)

◈ 3/4 yd. tan print for background

◈ 1/4 yd. red print for inner border

◈ 1 5/8 yds. backing (see note above with
directional print)

◈ 3/8 yds. binding

Set of 4 placemats:

◈ 8" x 15" piece of blue plaid for the roofs

◈ 1/4 yd. blue print for the houses and border

◈ 6" x 20" piece of green print #1 for treetops

◈ 6" x 20" piece of green print #2 for windows and
tree branches

◈ 1/2 yd. green print #3 for the tree branches and
outer border

◈ 6" x 20" piece of green print #4 for tree branches

◈ 6" x 14" piece of green print #5 for tree trunks,
chimneys and doors

◈ 5/8 yd. light print

◈ 1 yd. backing

◈ 5/8 yd. binding

Cutting Instructions:

All instructions given for these projects are for rotary cutting. You may then piece either by hand or machine. Mark and label the uses and sizes of the pieces as you cut them as many dimensions are small and close in size. It would be easy to confuse them when sewing.

Cutting for the table runner:

From the red stripe, cut:

◆ 8 - 3 1/2" x 6 1/2" rectangles for the roofs

From the blue check, cut:

◆ 8 - 1 1/2" x 6 1/2" pieces for house piecing

◆ 32 - 1 1/4" x 2" pieces for house piecing

◆ 16 - 1" x 3" pieces for house piecing

◆ 4 - 2" x 42" strips for outer border

From the gold print, cut:

◆ 16 - 1 1/2" x 2" pieces for windows

From the red print, cut:

◆ 8 - 1 1/2" x 2 1/2" pieces for doors

From the brown print #1, cut:

◆ 8 - 1 1/2" x 3" pieces for the chimneys

From 1 of the 4 green prints, cut:

◆ 12 - 2 1/2" x 4 1/2" rectangles for treetops

From each of the other 3 green prints, cut:

◆ 12 - 1 1/2" x 4 1/2" rectangles for tree branches

From the brown print #2, cut:

◆ 12 - 1" x 1 1/2" pieces for tree trunks

From the stripe print, cut:

◆ 1 strip, 2 1/2" x 30 1/2" for the road

From the light print, cut:

◆ 8 - 3 1/2" squares for roof piecing

◆ 4 - 3 7/8" squares, cut ◰ for chimney piecing

◆ 24 - 1 1/2" x 2 1/4" rectangles for tree trunk piecing

◆ 4 - 1 1/2" x 6 1/2" strips for quilt assembly

◆ 3 - 1 1/2" x 42" strips, crosscut into 72 squares for tree branch piecing

◆ 2 - 2 1/2" x 42" strips crosscut into 24 squares for treetop piecing

From the red border print, cut:

◆ 4 - 1 1/2" x 42" strips

Cutting for the 4 placemats:

From the blue plaid, cut:

◆ 4 - 3 1/2" x 6 1/2" rectangles

From the blue print, cut:

◆ 4 - 1 1/2" x 6 1/2" pieces for house piecing

◆ 16 - 1 1/4" x 2" pieces for house piecing

◆ 8 - 1" x 3" pieces for house piecing

◆ 8 - 1 1/2" x 9 1/2" strips for side borders

◆ 8 - 1 1/2" x 16 1/2" strips for top and bottom borders

From the green print #1, cut:

◆ 8 - 2 1/2" x 4 1/2" rectangles for treetops

From the green print #2, cut:

◆ 8 - 1 1/2" x 4 1/2" rectangles for tree branches

◆ 8 - 1 1/2" x 2" pieces for windows

From the green print #3, cut:

◆ 8 - 1 1/2" x 4 1/2" rectangles for tree branches

◆ 8 - 2" x 11 1/2" strips for side borders

◆ 8 - 2" x 19 1/2" strips for top and bottom borders

From the green print #4, cut:
- 8 - 1 1/2" x 4 1/2" rectangles for tree branches

From the green print #5, cut:
- 4 - 1 1/2" x 3" pieces for the chimneys
- 4 - 1 1/2" x 2 1/2" pieces for the doors
- 8 - 1" x 1 1/2" pieces for the tree trunks

From the light print, cut,
- 4 - 3 1/2" squares for roof piecing
- 2 - 3 7/8" squares, cut  for chimney piecing
- 16 - 1 1/2" x 2 1/4" rectangles for tree trunk piecing
- 2 - 1 1/2" x 42" strips, crosscut into 48 squares for tree branch piecing
- 1 - 2 1/2" x 42" strip crosscut into 16 squares for treetop piecing
- 8 - 2" x 14 1/2" strips for placemat piecing

Assembly Instructions

Refer to special skills on:
- Folded Corners on p. 25
- Integrated Piecing on p. 31

House Block

1. Referring to Folded Corners on p. xx, draw a diagonal line from corner to corner on the wrong side of each a light 3 1/2" square.

2. Place a square with right sides together on the left corner of the roof rectangle as shown. Stitch on the drawn line, fold, trim and press.

3. Cut a 1 1/2" strip from the side of a 3 7/8" light triangle orienting the triangle as shown. Insert a 1 1/2" x 3" chimney rectangle between the two light pieces as shown.

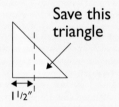

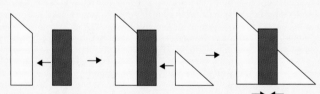

4. Trim the pieced triangle to 3 1/2" as shown. If you have a triangle trimmer, use it. If not, use a regular ruler to measure and trim the short sides to 3 1/2" as shown.

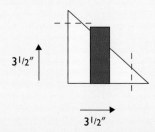

5. Use the 1/4" line on your regular rotary ruler to trim the long diagonal edge. Place the 1/4" line on the 3 1/2" corners you made in step 4 and trim away the excess beyond the ruler edge. This creates a 1/4" seam allowance on the diagonal edge.If you pieced by hand, secure each cut seam with a backstitch and knot just inside the cut edge. This will prevent the hand stitching from unraveling.

Trim ¼" away from corners to create a ¼" seam allowance along the long edge

6. Sew the pieced chimney triangle to the other side of the roof.

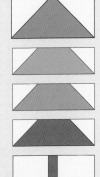

7. Using the roof units from above, the windows, the doors and the assorted house-piecing units, assemble a house as shown.

1½" x 2"   1¼" x 2"

1¼" x 2"

1" x 3"

Door 1½" x 2½"

1½" x 6½"

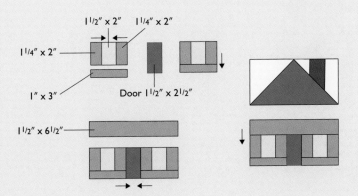

8. Repeat Steps 1-7 to make 8 houses for the table runner or 4 houses for the set of placemats.

Tree Block

1. Draw a diagonal line on the wrong side of 2 - 2 1/2" light squares. Sew, trim and press the marked square to the top of a green 2 1/2" x 4 1/2" rectangle to make a treetop.

2. In the same fashion, mark, sew, trim and press 2 - 1 1/2" light squares to the corners of a green print 1 1/2" x 4 1/2" rectangles to make a tree branch. Repeat the process with the other 2 green print tree branches for a total of 3 different color tree branches.

3. Sew a 1 1/2" x 2 1/4" light strip to opposite sides of a 1" x 1 1/2" tree trunk.

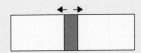

4. Assemble a tree block as shown.

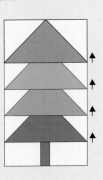

5. Repeat Steps 1-4 to make 12 Tree blocks for the table runner or 8 for the placemat set.

Finishing the Table Runner

1. Sew 4 houses together alternately with 3 trees to make one side of the street. Make 2 sets.

2. Sew the house and tree strips to either side of the road strip being careful to orient the houses correctly on either side of the street.

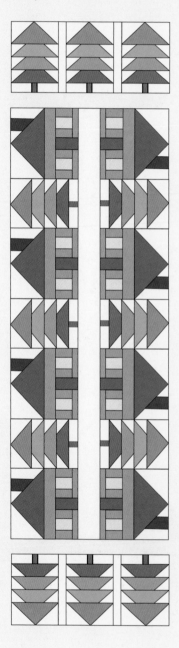

3. Sew 3 tree blocks together alternately with 2 light 1 1/2" x 6 1/2" strips. Make 2 sets. Sew the tree units to either end of the house/road unit.

4. Following the general directions on p. 35 for Plain Borders, sew the red borders to the quilt, followed by the blue borders.

5. Layer, baste and quilt as desired.

6. Bind with 8 - 2 1/4"-wide cross-grain double fold binding strips.

. . . .

Finishing the Placemats

1. Sew a tree to either side of a house block. Make 4.

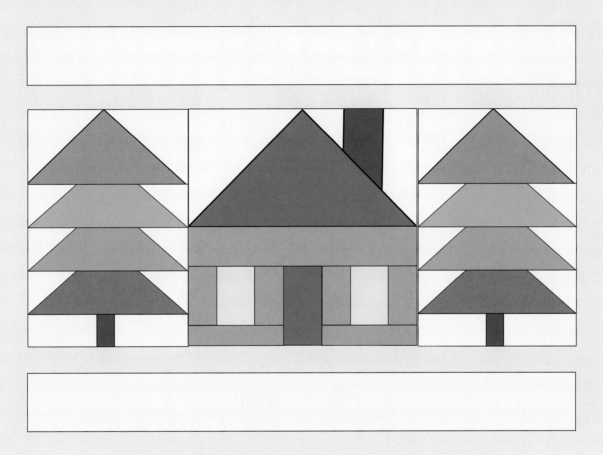

2. Sew a 2" x 14 1/2" light strip to the top and bottom of each house/tree unit.

3. Following the general directions on p. 35 for Plain Borders, sew the blue borders to the quilt, followed by the green borders.

4. Layer, baste and quilt as desired.

5. Bind each placemat with 2 - 2 1/4"-wide cross-grain double fold binding strips.

Nine-Patch Squared 🧵

Quilt Size: 48" square
Hand and machine pieced by Donna Lynn Thomas, Basehor, KS,
machine quilted by Sandy Gore, Liberty, MO 2007

This is a great beginner block for hand piecing. It starts with a simple nine-patch in the center and moves on to an assortment of triangles using an easy assembly process.

Nine-Patch Squared

Block size: 12" finished size

Number of blocks: 9

Fabric Requirements:

- ◈ 5/8 yd. green batik for outer border and block piecing
- ◈ 5/8 yd. red print for inner border and block piecing
- ◈ 3/8 yd. medium green print for block piecing
- ◈ 5/8 yd. orange/gold print for block piecing
- ◈ 3/4 yd. cream print for block piecing
- ◈ 3/8 yd. light green print for block piecing
- ◈ 3/8 yd. for binding
- ◈ 3 3/8 yds. for backing

Cutting Instructions:

From the green batik, cut:
- ◈ 24 Template A
- ◈ 4 strips, 4" x 42" for outer borders

From the red print, cut:
- ◈ 21 Template A
- ◈ 4 strips 2 1/2" x 42" for inner borders

From the medium green print, cut:
- ◈ 36 Template D

From the orange/gold print, cut:
- ◈ 36 Template B

From the cream print, cut:
- ◈ 36 Template C

From the light green print, cut:
- ◈ 36 Template A

Assembly Instructions:

1. Using 4 red squares, 4 light green squares, and the 5 green batik squares, assemble the 2 types of nine-patches shown. Make 5 Type A and 4 Type B.

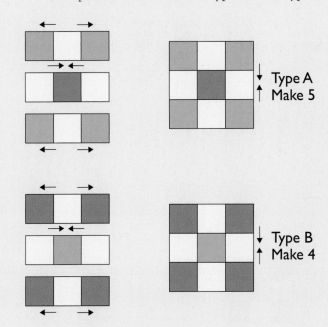

Type A
Make 5

Type B
Make 4

2. Sew an orange/gold triangle to each side of the nine-patch unit.

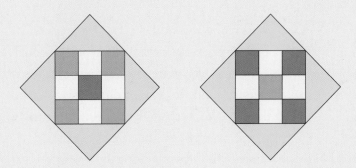

3. Sew a medium green triangle to each cream Template C. Sew the green/cream units to the 4 sides of all 9 blocks. Be careful to press in the directions of the arrows.

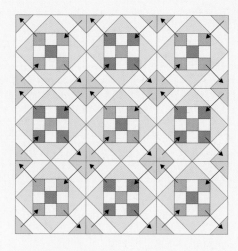

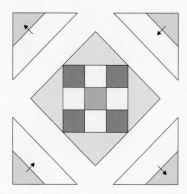

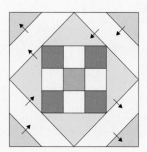 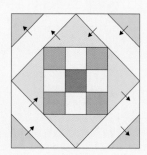

4. Sew the blocks together in a 3 x 3 set as shown. Note the placement of the 2 different nine-patch centers. Carefully orient the pressing of the green corners according to pressing direction as shown in the diagram. By carefully following the pressing plan, the diagonal seams of the blocks should butt where they meet, making the sewing process easier.

5. Following the general instructions on p. 35 for Plain Borders, sew the red and green batik borders in place to complete the quilt top.

6. Layer, baste and quilt as desired.

7. Bind with 5 - 2 1/4"-wide cross-grain double fold binding strips.